79 AMAZING SCIENCE GAMES

to Blow Your Mind!

ANNA CLAYBOURNE

ARCTURUS

This edition published in 2022 by Arcturus Publishing Limited
26/27 Bickels Yard, 151–153 Bermondsey Street,
London SE1 3HA

Author: Anna Claybourne
Illustrator: Amy Wilcox
Editor: Susie Rae
Designer: Jeni Child
Design Manager: Jessica Holliland
Editorial Manager: Joe Harris

ISBN: 978-1-3988-1526-1
CH010106NT
Supplier 29, Date 0822, PI 00002154

Printed in China

What is STEM?

STEM is a world-wide initiative that
aims to cultivate an interest in
Science, Technology, Engineering, and
Mathematics, in an effort to promote
these disciplines to as wide a variety
of students as possible.

CONTENTS

INTRODUCTION

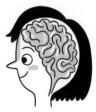

In these pages are dozens of fantastic science challenges, activities, and games to play with your friends, family, and class. But before we get started, let's ask an important question:

What is science?

Science is a way of finding out about the world. Scientists make predictions about how things work, and then test them to find out whether they are true.

But science doesn't have to be serious! As this book will show, you can use science to build cool contraptions, take part in contests, try out incredible experiments, and amaze your friends.

But science does matter.

That's because we also use science to understand the world around us, come up with inventions, and make all kinds of everyday things work.

Rockets going to space depend on rocket science!

... and we have to understand materials to build skyscrapers and bridges that won't fall down.

We need to know about forces to make cars, trains, and planes ...

Many kinds of science go into making computers and robots.

... and understanding DNA helps us detect diseases, make medicines, and catch criminals!

The science of chemistry helps us make all kinds of things— from paints and batteries to sewage treatment plants ...

Let the games begin!

The science games in this book will help you discover all kinds of amazing facts, and enjoy doing some cool experiments yourself.

You can explore how magnets work, why things float, why some seeds have wings, how your brain sends signals, how your memory works, what DNA is made of, and much more!

... games to play on your own or with a friend ...

There are games you can play with just a paper and pencil ...

... games you can play on a walk or car ride ...

... games that are great for a big group, in a classroom, or at a science party!

Ready to play?
Let's go!

MYSTERIOUS MARBLES

This game is about making predictions. Can you guess what will happen when the marbles collide? Challenge a friend and see who gets it right!

What do you need?

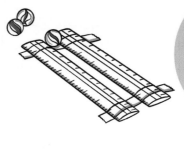

- At least five marbles, all the same size
- Something to roll them along, so they stay in a straight line, such as a ruler with a channel along the middle, or you can line up two rulers side-by-side
- Use tape or sticky tack to keep your channel in place

Play on your own or with any number of people.

How to play

1 Put a row of three marbles in the middle of the channel, touching each other.

2 Put another marble a little distance away.

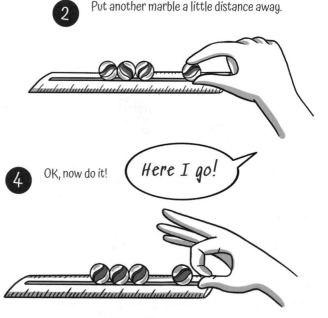

3 Flick it gently toward the others, so that it hits the one on the end. But before you do, STOP! What do you think is going to happen? If you're playing with someone else, or have a parent or sibling around, ask them what they think will happen too.

4 OK, now do it!

Here I go!

People often think all the marbles will move. In fact, if you did it right, only the one on the other end of the row will roll away!

Try this too!

What happens if you have a longer row of marbles?

What if you roll two marbles together toward the others?

Game science

The famous scientist Isaac Newton, and several other scientists, studied this effect in the 1600s.

The rolling marble is carrying movement energy (called kinetic energy). That energy gets passed on to the first marble in the row, which passes it on to the next, and so on. Only the one at the end rolls away, as there's nothing to stop it.

If you roll two marbles, they carry more energy and make two marbles roll away.

Fascinating!

This toy, called a Newton's cradle, works the same way.

MARBLE TRAMPOLINES

Do you love bouncing on a trampoline? Make this mini version for a marble to bounce on!

Woohoo!

Experiment on your own, or make up challenges and play against friends or family.

What do you need?

- A few marbles
- A pack of round balloons
- Scissors
- Several old jars or small plastic food containers (don't use fancy cups or glasses, in case they get damaged)

Set it up

1 To make the trampolines, you need a balloon for each jar or container. Neatly cut off the neck of each balloon, where it starts to get wider.

2 Stretch each balloon over a jar or container. Pull down the sides firmly so the top is stretched flat and smooth.

How to play

 3 Drop a marble onto a trampoline so that it bounces. Try dropping it from higher up. How high can you make it bounce? It will work best if you can get it to land right in the middle.

 4 Once you've got the hang of it, try these challenges:

How many times can you make one marble bounce on the same trampoline? →

Can you bounce a marble off a trampoline and into a plastic bowl? ←

Can you set up several trampolines of different heights in a row and make a marble bounce "down the steps"? →

Game science

How do trampolines work? It's another case of energy science!

Like real trampolines, balloons are made of stretchy material. When the marble lands on it, its kinetic energy pushes the balloon and makes it stretch. This stores the energy in the stretched balloon. Then it springs back, pushing the energy back into the marble and ...

BOINNNGGG!

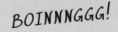

On a real trampoline, the same thing happens with the stretchy springs around the edge.

BOINNNGGG!

9

VISCOSITY RACE

What's viscosity? You're about to find out! It's time to get the marbles out again—but this time they're going diving ...

What do you need?

- At least three small, clear jars or glasses, all the same size
- The same number of marbles, also all the same size
- A selection of different liquids, such as water, dish soap, clear shampoo or shower gel, honey, cooking oil, and salt water (warm water with several teaspoons of salt stirred in)

Hey! That's my shampoo!

This is best with at least two people, so you can drop the marbles all at once.

How to play

1 Line up your jars or glasses in a row. Then fill each one with a different liquid. For example, if you have three jars or glasses, you could fill one with water, one with oil, and one with shampoo. Make sure you fill them all to the same level.

Honey   Water   Oil

2 Next, you're going to drop a marble into each jar. But before you do, how fast do you think the marbles will sink? Guess which one will land at the bottom first, next, and last. Get the other players to guess, too.

3 Now, with a friend to help, hold the three marbles just above the top of each jar, right in the middle.

On the count of three ... let go!

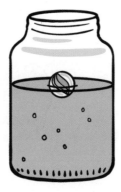

What happened? Did you get it right?

Game science

As you pour the liquids into the jars, you'll notice that some are thicker than others, and move slower. Scientists call this viscosity. The more viscous a liquid is, the more slowly it pours, and the more slowly objects move through it.

A liquid's viscosity depends on what it's made of, how close together its atoms and molecules are, and how they behave.

ROCKET BALLOON

5, 4, 3, 2, 1 ... we have balloon blastoff!

What do you need?

- A balloon for each person
- Lots of thin string or strong thread
- A paper straw (or make your own by rolling paper into a tube)
- Scissors
- Tape
- Fixed, sturdy objects to tie the string to, such as coat hooks, banisters, or window locks (don't use furniture, as it could move)

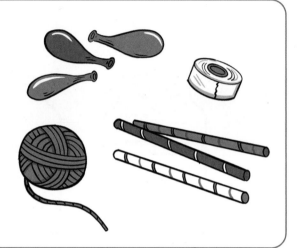

How to play

1 If your straw has a bendy section, cut it off, leaving just a straight piece.

This is lots of fun for any number of people!

2 Ask an adult to help you tie a piece of string to a fixed object such as a banister. Thread the straw onto the string, then tie the other end of the string somewhere else, making sure it's pulled tight and straight. It can be level or sloping.

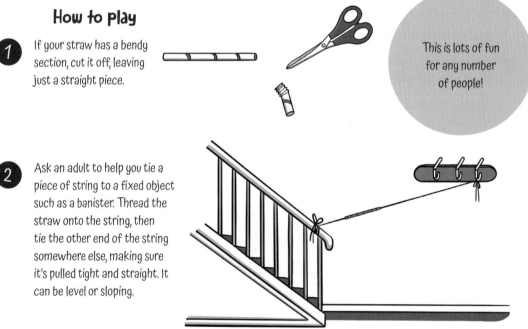

3 Blow up a balloon, then hold it closed (or use a peg or food bag clip to hold it closed). Tape the balloon to the piece of straw. You may need to ask someone to help you with this step.

If the string is sloping, put the balloon at the lower end.

Make sure the open end of the balloon is at one end of the string.

4 When you're ready for liftoff, let go!

Whoosh!

The rocket balloon should zoom along the string.

Try this too!

If you have enough space, you could set up two strings side-by-side and have a rocket race! Or try setting up the longest string you can, and see how far your balloon rocket will go.

Game science

As the air shoots out of the balloon, the balloon and the air push away from each other.

The balloon gets pushed this way ...

... as the air gets pushed this way.

The same thing happens when a real space rocket burns fuel.

... as lots of gas pushes downward out of the rocket!

The rocket gets pushed up ...

MAGIC BOTTLE DIVER

Make a mini diver that can rise up and down inside a bottle full of water
without anything touching it—as if by magic! (It's not magic, though. It's science!)

Make this
on your own
or as a team.

How to play

1 Fill up your bottle with cold tap water, right to
the top. Place it in a basin to catch any spills.

2 Use your dropper to suck up a little bit of water,
so the tube is about half-full.

What do you need?

- A large, clear plastic bottle
  with a screw-on lid
- Water
- A eye dropper. Or, if you don't
  have a dropper, you can use
  an unopened plastic sauce
  sachet, like the ones you get
  in restaurants

3 Put the dropper into the bottle. It should float and bob around near the top. A little water may spill out of the bottle—that's OK.

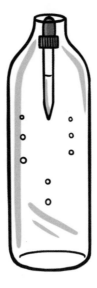

4 Screw on the bottle lid tightly.

Game science

How does it work? When you squeeze the bottle, water pushes on the air inside the diver, squishing it and making it take up less space. That makes the diver denser, or heavier for its size, and it sinks. When you release the pressure, the air expands and takes up more space again—and the diver rises!

And back up we go!

5 To make the diver dive, put one or both hands around the bottle and gently squeeze it. If nothing happens, squeeze a bit harder. This should make the diver dive down to the bottom ...

6 ... and when you let go, it rises back up!

GRAVITY GUESSING GAME

If you drop something light and something heavy at the same time,
which will hit the ground first—and why?

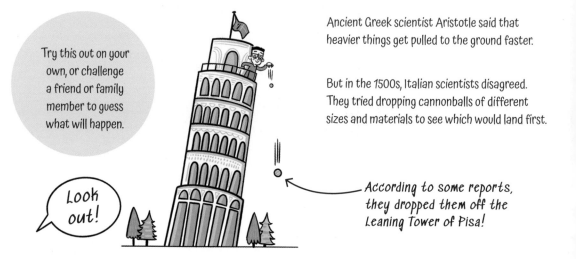

Try this out on your own, or challenge a friend or family member to guess what will happen.

Look out!

Ancient Greek scientist Aristotle said that heavier things get pulled to the ground faster.

But in the 1500s, Italian scientists disagreed. They tried dropping cannonballs of different sizes and materials to see which would land first.

According to some reports, they dropped them off the Leaning Tower of Pisa!

What do you need?

- Tissue or toilet paper
- A metal coin
- Scissors
- Two identical small boxes, such as matchboxes or small food containers with lids

How to play

1 Do this indoors, where there's no wind, as the air needs to be completely still.

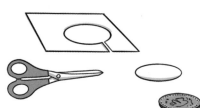

2 Cut out a circle of tissue paper the same size as the coin.

3 Hold the coin and circle of paper in front of you at the same height.

4 Count to three and then drop them at the exact same time.

5 The paper should take much longer to reach the ground—but why? Is it because they are different weights, as Aristotle said?

6 You can test this out by putting the objects into the two identical containers. Now they are still different weights, as the paper is still lighter—but they are the exact same shape.

7 Repeat the experiment again and see what happens!

Game science

When the objects are in the boxes, they should land at the same time. That's because gravity pulls objects at the same speed, no matter how big, small, light, or heavy they are!

The reason the paper falls slower the first time is air resistance. The lighter paper circle is slowed down more by air pushing up on it, like a parachute. But if there wasn't any air there, it would shoot straight down to the ground, just like the coin.

THUD!   THUD!

CANDLE SEESAW

Make a seesaw that moves up and down by itself—thanks to the power of fire.

What do you need?

- A large baking tray, or a normal tray covered in foil
- Two identical, unused birthday cake candles
- Tape
- A sewing needle (a longer one if possible)
- Two identical glasses
- Matches or a lighter

Always ask an adult to watch and help when you're doing anything with candles or flames.

How to play

1 Hold the bases of two candles together, like this, and wrap tape around them to hold them firmly.

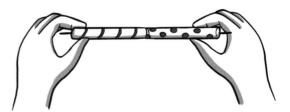

2 Ask an adult to push the needle through the middle of the tape, right where the two candles meet.

3 Place your two glasses in the middle of the tray, about 2.5 cm (1 in) apart, and balance the needle between them.

4 Then ask an adult to light both candles—first one, then the other a few seconds later.

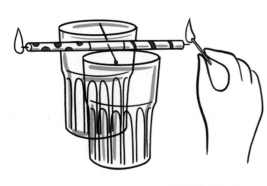

5 Sit back and see what happens!

Game science

If it works, the candles should start to seesaw. As each candle burns, wax melts and drips onto the tray. Each time a candle drips, it gets slightly lighter and the other candle moves down—until it drips too, and moves up again.

Wheeee!

Woohoo!

The movement couldn't keep going on its own. It can only happen because the candles are lit, making the wax melt and causing movement.

Remember!

Don't leave your candle seesaw burning without anyone there, and make sure you blow the candles out before they burn down to the tape.

MAGIC CABBAGE JUICE

It's time for another guessing game! You'll be amazed to see cabbage juice change from purple to pink or blue before your very eyes.

Set it up

1 Tear the cabbage leaves into small pieces and put them in the bowl. Ask an adult to add hot tap water until the cabbage is just covered.

2 Use the wooden spoon to squash and mash the cabbage in the water for about five minutes.

3 Ask an adult to strain the water into the pitcher. It will be dark purple, so it's a good idea to do this in the kitchen sink in case of spills.

What do you need?

- A small red cabbage
- A large bowl
- Wooden spoon
- Sieve or strainer
- A large pitcher
- 4–10 small clear or white glasses or containers, or paper cups
- Substances to test, such as: lemon juice, vinegar, baking soda, salt, sugar, milk, fizzy drinks, or shampoo

This involves hot water, so you need an adult to help with that part.

You can do this on your own (with an adult to help, of course!) or with friends or family.

4 Half-fill your your small glasses or containers with cabbage water.

How to play

5 To test your substances, add each one to a different container of cabbage water. Before you put them in, try to predict what will happen.

6 If it's a liquid, such as lemon juice, add a few drops. If nothing happens, add a bit more.

Game science

Red cabbage water is a natural pH indicator, or acid test. It changes when it mixes with two different types of chemicals: acids and alkalis. Acids, like lemon juice and vinegar, turn it pink or red. Alkalis, like baking soda, turn it blue or green.

Scientists use indicators like this to find out how acidic or alkaline chemicals are.

7 For solids like baking powder, sugar, or salt, add a couple of teaspoonfuls and stir.

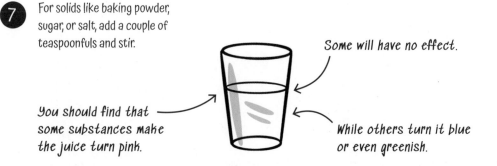

Some will have no effect.

You should find that some substances make the juice turn pink.

While others turn it blue or even greenish.

8 As you try out more substances, do you get better at predicting the results?

COPTER LAUNCHER

Turn a piece of cardboard into a simple flying machine and launch it into the air! The angled folds in the paper create lift.

Play on your own, or make a launcher for each person and compete to fly the highest.

How to play

1 Measure and cut out a rectangle of thin cardboard about 10 cm (4 in) long and 5 cm (2 in) wide. Fold down the two opposite corners.

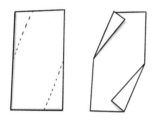

What do you need?

- Thin craft cardboard, or a food package such as a cereal box
- Ruler
- Pointed scissors
- Three sharp, full-length pencils
- Strong tape

2 Now take your three pencils and wrap tape around the ends of the pencils to hold them firmly together, like this.

3 Press the two pencil tips onto the middle of the cardboard to make two dots. Use the point of your scissors to carefully make two small holes where the dots are (ask an adult to help with this if you like).

4 To use the launcher, hold it with the two pencils pointing up and balance your piece of cardboard on top with the pencil points in the two holes.

5 Hold the single pencil at the bottom between the palms of your hands and quickly roll it to make the launcher spin.

It will only work in one direction—you'll have to figure out which!

MINI SPINNER

If you only have a few minutes, make this smaller spinner instead.

How to play

 1 Measure and cut out a piece of paper 12 cm (5 in) long and 5 cm (2 in) wide.

 2 Use the pencil and ruler to draw lines on it, like this.

 3 Then cut along these three lines with the scissors.

 4 On the lower end of the paper, fold in the two sides, fold the bottom up, then hold it in place with the paper clip.

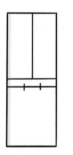

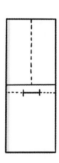

 5 Then fold down the two flaps at the top in opposite directions.

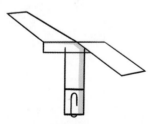

 6 To make it spin, simply drop it!

23

MAGNET QUIZ

Do you know which things will stick to a magnet? Time to test it out ...

How to play

 1 Collect your objects, then put them in a pile.

Will stick	Won't stick
Coin	

2 Each person should then write two lists on a piece of paper—the things they think will stick to a magnet, and the things that won't.

3 When everyone has finished, test the objects by touching them with the magnet. Which ones does it pull on? How many did you get right?

Game science

Magnets only pull on a few particular substances. The most common are iron, steel (which is mostly made of iron), and two other metals: cobalt and nickel.

A coin, for example, will stick to a magnet if it contains quite a lot of nickel, but not if it's made of copper.

Can't get me!

What do you need?

- A magnet
- Pencil and paper
- A selection of household objects, such as:

  Pencil

  Eraser

  Coins

  Paperclips

  Teaspoon

  Scissors

  Plastic brick

  String

  Paintbrush

  Tape measure

  Marble

SINK OR SWIM?

This game is similar to the previous one, but this time you're testing to see what will float.

This is best for two or more players.

How to play

 1 Collect your objects. Each person should make lists of which they think will sink in water, and which will float.

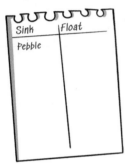

Sink	Float
Pebble	

2 When everyone's ready, run water into the sink, or put the bowl on the floor and pour in the water using a pitcher until it's about 7 cm (3 in) deep.

 3 One at time, test each object by dropping it gently into the water. Who was right?

4 Count up who got the most right to find a winner!

What do you need?

- A kitchen sink, or a large plastic bowl and a pitcher
- Water
- A selection of objects that can get wet, such as:

  Eraser

  Coin

  Teaspoon

  Plastic brick

  Marble

  Dice

  Wood block

  Pebble

Game science

Objects float if they are less dense, or heavy for their size, than water. So, for example, if a wooden dice is lighter than the exact same amount of water, it will float. The least dense materials, like cork, float the highest. The most dense materials sink!

SINK THE SHIP!

How good are you at shipbuilding? Design and make a boat that will be the last to sink!

This is a game for two or more players.

How to play

1 If you're using a sink or bathtub, fill it with water to about 10 cm (4 in) deep. If you're using a bowl, put it somewhere like on a bathroom or kitchen floor, or outdoors, where it won't matter if some water splashes out. Then fill it with water to 10 cm (4 in) deep.

What do you need?

- Kitchen foil
- Scissors
- Tape measure or ruler
- A sink or bathtub, or a large plastic bowl
- Water
- Lots of coins, marbles, paperclips, or other weights

Make sure an adult is there to supervise if you're using the bathtub.

2 Cut or tear off a piece of foil the same length for each player. Around 30 cm (12 in) long is a good size.

3 Now for the ships! Each person has to shape and bend their foil to make a little boat that will float on the water. You're trying to make the strongest, sturdiest boat you can, one that will hold as much weight as possible without sinking.

4 When everyone has made a boat, float them on the water.

5 Everyone has to take a matching weight, such as coins that are all the same type and size. On the count of three, put your weight into your boat.

6 Keep doing this to load the boats with more cargo. You can use different types of weights, but they must all be the same on each try, to make it fair.

Swim with the fishes!

Eventually, the boats will start to sink. Whose will be the last one afloat?

Game science

To float, a boat has to be less dense (heavy for its size) than water. The foil is made of metal, which is denser than water—but when you make it into a boat shape, the air inside makes it less dense, so it floats.

But adding the weights increases the density, until the boat can't float any more. Try spreading your weights out evenly around your boat, so that it stays level and doesn't sink until the last moment!

PENDULUM SKITTLES

If you've ever been ten-pin bowling, you'll know it's pretty hard to knock all the pins over. But maybe it would be easier if the ball was on a string ...

This game works best with two or more players.

What do you need?

- String
- Scissors
- A door frame
- Tape or a thumbtack or drawing pin
- A smallish ball, such as a rubber bouncy ball or tennis ball
- 6-10 cardboard tubes or empty plastic bottles to use as skittles

How to play

1 Cut a piece of string about 2 m (7 ft) long. Tie one end of it around your ball, and use tape to make sure the string is firmly attached.

2 Ask an adult to help attach the other end of the string to the middle of a door frame. They can either tape it on, or (if it's OK to make a hole), use a thumbtack or drawing pin. The ball should hang down to about 10 cm (4 in) off the floor.

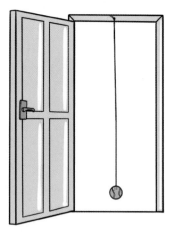

3 Now hold the ball to one side and stand your cardboard tube or plastic bottle skittles in the doorway. You can put them in a row, or in a pattern such as a triangle.

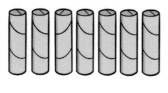

 4 To play, take the ball, hold it away from the skittles, then let it go or give it a push. Your aim is to make it swing to and fro in a way that knocks over all the skittles.

 5 If it doesn't work, how many attempts does it take you to get them all?

6 Set up the skittles again for each player, and see who can knock all the skittles down in the fewest tries.

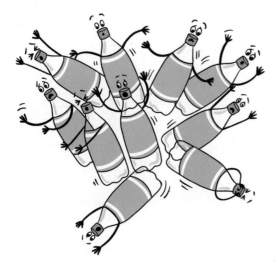

Game science

Your ball on a string is also known as a pendulum. If you let it swing straight, it will move to and fro in a line. If you give it a push to the side, it will move around in an oval shape, which could hit more skittles!

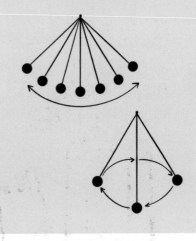

PENNY PUSHER

Make yourself a board and play the traditional game of shove ha'penny.

What do you need?

- Large piece of thick cardboard
- Ruler
- Marker pen
- Scissors
- Five coins, all the same size and type
- Paper to record your scores

This can be played by two people, or you could play in teams.

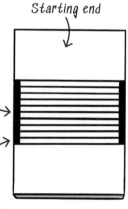

How to play

1 Mark a rectangle on the cardboard, 50 cm (20 in) long and 13 cm (5 in) wide. (If your cardboard isn't that big, you can make it a bit smaller.) Cut it out carefully (ask an adult to help if you like).

2 Now measure the width of the coins you're using. Write the measurement down, and add 6 mm (0.25 in).

18 mm + 6 mm = 24 mm

3 Now use this result to measure and draw ten straight lines across the middle of the board. If your result was 25 mm (1 in), make them 25 mm (1 in) apart.

Start in the middle, then add lines on each side until you have ten

Starting end

Fill in two strips 1 cm (0.4 in) wide along the edges.

4. Take all five coins and put them at the starting end of the board.

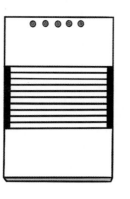

5. Push or flick the coins with your finger, one at a time, so they slide over the lines.

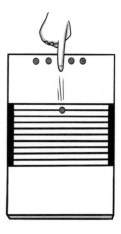

6. Try to get the coins into the spaces between the lines without touching a line. If a coin is on a line, aim the next coin to try to shove it into a gap.

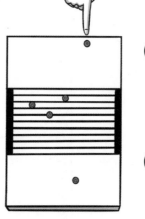

7. If a coin goes past the last line, it's out of the game.

8. After you've shoved all five coins, count how many are in the spaces between the lines and write down your score.

9. Then it's the other player's turn!

Game science

This game works because of friction, a force that slows or stops objects as they rub together. As the coins slide over the cardboard, friction makes them slow down and stop. You have to use exactly the right amount of force so they stop in the right place!

MARBLE TARGETS

Can you control where a marble goes
by hitting it with another marble?

This is best for
two players.

How to play

1 Put your piece of paper or thin
cardboard on the flat surface.

2 Measure and cut out five strips
of cardboard, each about 5 cm
(2 in) wide and 15 cm (6 in) long.

3 Bend the strips into curved shapes,
and tape them to one end of your
piece of paper in a row to make
little targets.

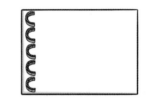

What do you need?

- A flat, smooth surface,
  such as a dinner table
- Large piece of flat,
  smooth paper or thin
  cardboard
- Thick cardboard, such
  as an old packing box
- Ruler
- Scissors
- Tape
- Pen or pencil
- At least two marbles

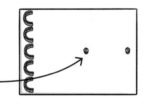

4 Now, draw two small circles on the
paper, one in the middle and one at
the empty end.

Put one marble in each circle.

5 To play a turn, ask the other player
to pick one of the five targets. You
have to flick the marble at the end
so it hits the middle one and makes
it hit the right target.

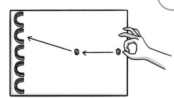

*Take turns and
see who can get
the highest score!*

Game science

To make the middle marble go in the right direction, you have to hit it
at the right angle. If you make the first marble glance off one side of
it, it will push it in the opposite direction, like this.

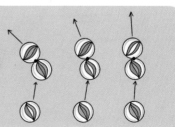

It takes practice to get it right—keep trying!

TIDDLYWINKS

Squidge a wink with a squidger, and flip it into the bowl!

What do you need?

- A smooth flat surface
- Small bowl or pot to use as a target
- Plastic game counters or flat plastic buttons

This game is for two or more players.

How to play

1 All you have to do is take one counter or button, the "wink," and press (or squidge) it on the edge with another one, the "squidger," to make it flip up in the air.

2 Once you've got the hang of it, aim for the target and see how many each player can get in!

Game science

When you press the edge of a tiddlywink, it gets squeezed, then springs back and jumps!

MAGNET SOCCER

Try your skills at magic magnetic soccer, with this easy-to-make game.

This is another two-player game.

How to play

 Take your cardboard box and find a flat, smooth side with no flaps or gaps. Draw a line around this side of the box, about 5 cm (2 in) from the edge.

2 Carefully cut along the line to cut the side off the box. Tape down any loose parts. This is your soccer field! If you like, you can mark it with lines, like this.

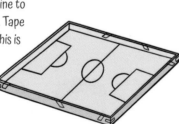

3 Using the leftover cardboard, cut out six circles 4 cm (1.5 in) across. Glue them together in threes to make your players. Use marker pens to make one player red and the other blue.

What do you need?

- Cardboard packing box
- Small cardboard box, such as a food package
- Black, red, and blue marker pens
- Scissors
- Tape
- Two rulers
- Glue
- Four strong, disk-shaped magnets
- A marble

4 Tape one magnet under each circle shape, and one magnet onto the end of each ruler. Check the magnets on the rulers and circles pull toward each other—if they don't, flip one of them over.

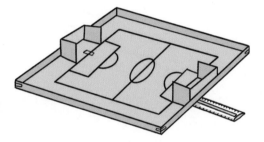

5 Cut your small cardboard box in half and use the halves to make two goals. Stick them to opposite ends of your pitch.

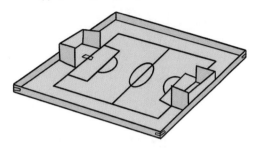

6 Ask an adult to help you cut a slot in the side of the box behind each goal, big enough for your rulers to fit through.

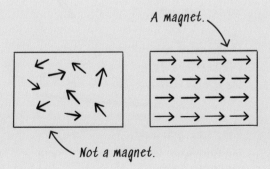

7 Now, each player chooses a circle, then uses their ruler to control it from under the field. Put a marble in the middle, and use your circle to try to push it into the other player's goal (while defending your own goal, of course).

Game science

Magnets seem like magic, but they're not. Everything is made of tiny atoms, which have their own tiny pulling forces. In most materials, they all point in different directions and cancel each other out. But in a magnet, they all point the same way. This makes a bigger pulling force that attracts other magnets and some types of metal.

A magnet.

Not a magnet.

WOBBLY HANDOVER

Can you control the wobbles to hand over the marble?

This game is for two players—but instead of playing against each other, you have to work together.

What do you need?

- Two long, thin sticks, such as bamboo garden poles. About 1 m (3 ft) is a good length.
- Two small plastic containers, such as empty dessert pots
- Strong tape
- A few marbles

How to play

1 Take a container and tape it to one end of one of the sticks.

The easiest way is to tape the end of the stick to the side or base of the container, then use lots more tape to wrap around the container and the stick to hold them firmly together.

2 Now do the same with the other container and stick, so you have one for each player.

If the stick has a thinner end, tape the cup to that end.

Make sure you leave the opening of the container clear.

I challenge you to a wobbly handover!

3 The aim of the game is for one player to pass the marble to the other, using only the sticks. Sounds simple—but it's harder than you think!

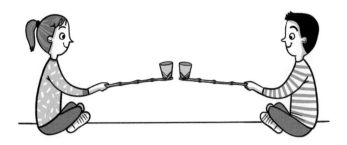

4 Sit facing each other so your sticks can just reach each other.

5 One player puts the marble in their container, then tries to drop it into the other player's container. To do this, you'll both need a very steady hand!

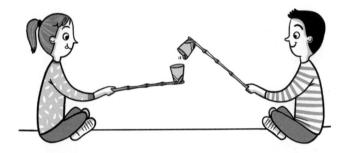

Game science

Why is it so hard? Well, when your hand is holding the stick, the stick acts like a lever. When you move your hand a little bit to change the stick's position, the other end moves a lot more!

This makes it very hard to control the other end of the stick and keep it still. With two of you both trying to control separate sticks, achieving the handover is a challenge—but it can be done! See how long it takes you to do it, then try again.

Steady ... steady!

SEED DESIGNER

What helps seeds fly away in the wind? Try designing your own to find out.

This game is for two or more players. If you have lots of people, you could work in teams.

Blowing in the wind

As you may have noticed, plant seeds often blow around in the wind. This helps them travel to a new place to grow, away from their parent plant, so they have more space. These seeds often have wing-shaped or fluffy parts to help them catch the wind.

Here are some of them ...

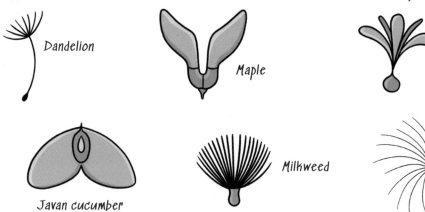

Burmese lacquer tree

Dandelion

Maple

Javan cucumber

Milkweed

Cotton grass

What do you need?

- Very small wooden or plastic buttons or beads, all the same size and shape, to use as seeds
- Thin and fluffy materials, such as cotton wool, plastic wrap, tissue paper, and feathers
- Sewing thread
- Scissors
- Glue
- An electric fan or hairdryer

Ask an adult if you can use the fan or hairdryer, and ask them to plug it in and turn it on for you.

How to play

 1 Give each person five bead or button "seeds." They have to add other materials to each seed to give it a fluffy parachute, wings, or whatever else they think will help it catch the wind.

2 When you've finished and let the glue dry, put your seeds to the test!

3 Ask an adult to turn on the fan, or hold the hairdryer and blow cold air. Take turns dropping your seeds into the wind and see how far they go.

Try making several different designs.

You could tie materials to your bead or button with thread, or use glue.

Don't use too much thread or glue, as it will make the bead heavier.

Who designed the winning seed?

Wheeeeee!

Game science

To catch the wind, seeds need something that has a big surface area but isn't too heavy. Lots of fluffy parts or thin, flat wings give the wind more surface area to push against and lift, helping the seed fly farther before it lands.

PAPER HOVERCRAFTS

Make these super-simple hovercrafts, then blow on them to make them zoom along.

This is a game for two or more players.

What do you need?

· Craft or printer paper

· Scissors

· A smooth floor or table

How to play

 Each player should make themselves a hovercraft to race. Start with a flat piece of paper. If it's not square, fold one corner over, then cut off the end to make a square.

 Now fold the square paper in half diagonally to make a triangle.

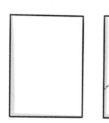

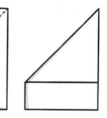 Fold that triangle in half to make a smaller triangle, then open it again.

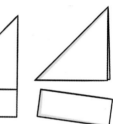

 Fold the two sides in to meet the middle, making a kite shape.

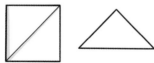

 Fold these flaps back on themselves. Flip the whole thing over, and your hovercraft is ready!

7 Now line up the hovercrafts in a row, ready to start the race. Each player should sit behind their hovercraft.

8 On the count of three, blow into the back of your hovercraft. They should zoom away—the one that goes the farthest distance is the winner!

Try this too!
You could try blowing into the hovercrafts using straws or cardboard tubes. Does it make them go faster or farther?

Game science

A real-life hovercraft uses a fan to pump air down into its lower section, or skirt. The air pushes down and shoots out around the edges, and this lifts the hovercraft, allowing it to glide over either water or the ground.

The paper hovercrafts are simpler, but they work in a similar way. When you blow into the hovercraft, air pressure builds up inside. To escape, the air pushes down and under the edges of the hovercraft, lifting it slightly off the ground. Without the friction with the ground to slow it down, it can scoot a long way!

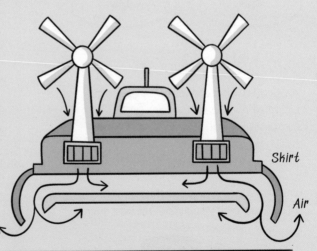

Skirt

Air

AQUA COIN

How many drops of water can you fit on a coin?
It's probably a lot more than you think ...

This game works best with two or more players.

How to play

1. Each person puts their coin on a plate in front of them.

2. Everyone then dips a straw or paintbrush into the cup or jar to pick up a drop of water, and carefully drops it onto their coin.

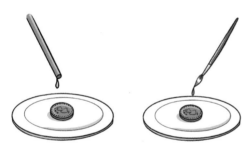

3. At first you'll have plenty of space, but soon your coin will be covered in water, and it will start to bulge up in a bubble-shaped dome.

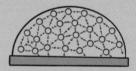

4. How long can you keep going before the water finally spills off your coin? Who could fit the most drops on their coin?

What do you need?

- A coin for each person (all the same type and size)
- A plate for each person to catch spills
- Straws or small paintbrushes
- Jar or cup of water

Game science

The water forms a dome because of a force called surface tension.

All the tiny molecules in water have weak pulling forces and pull on each other.

In the middle, they are pulled in all directions.

On the the surface, they are only pulled sideways and into the middle.

This pulls the surface molecules closer together, and they hold the rest of the water in like a kind of skin.

RACING FISH

Surface tension is the reason these fish race around!

For two or more players.

How to play

1 Put your tray on the floor or on a table, somewhere where a few spills won't matter. Pour water into the tray until it's about 1 cm (0.4 in) deep.

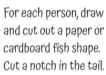

2 For each person, draw and cut out a paper or cardboard fish shape. Cut a notch in the tail.

3 Carefully put your fish in the water, lined up at one end of the tray.

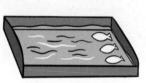

4 Put a blob of soap or shampoo on the small plate, then dip your matchstick or chopstick in it to pick up a drop. Dab it into the notch on your fish's tail.

Whose fish zooms through the water the fastest?

What do you need?

- Thick paper or thin cardboard
- Large, shallow, waterproof tray or baking tray
- Liquid soap or shampoo
- A chopstick or matchstick for each person
- Pitcher of water
- A small plate
- Pencil and scissors

Game science

What happened? Because of surface tension, the water molecules at the surface all pull toward each other. But soap breaks up the surface tension and stops it from working. When this happens, the molecules on the other side of the fish pull together even more, taking the fish with them.

SPACE SUIT TRIALS

When astronauts go on a spacewalk, they have to wear helmets, gloves, and space suits many layers thick—which makes it very hard to do tricky jobs like fixing spacecraft.

This game is for two or more players.

What do you need?

- Head-sized cardboard box
- Scissors
- Tape
- Wool hat or balaclava
- Three pairs of gloves
- Timer or stopwatch
- Items for tasks:

  A screw-top jar or container with three different coins inside

  Plastic construction bricks or wooden building blocks

  A needle and thread

... and I think this piece goes here!

1. To make your space helmet, cut a hole in one side of the cardboard box to look out of (but not while it's on your head!).

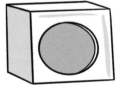

2 Each player now has to take turns wearing the hat or balaclava, the space helmet, and three pairs of gloves while trying to do the three tasks.

Unscrew the jar, take out the coins, and arrange them in a row from smallest to largest.

Use all the bricks or blocks to build a small wall or tower.

Thread the needle.

3 Time each player and see who can complete the tasks in the shortest time.

Game science

Why is it so hard? You don't think about it much, but you constantly rely on your sense of touch to help you hold and control everyday objects—especially in your fingers. When the gloves take that away, it's very hard to do tricky, fiddly tasks.

Our fingers contain thousands of touch-sensing nerves to help us feel and control objects.

Most of us also rely on our vision to help us do tricky tasks—so a big helmet getting in the way doesn't help!

Oops! Dropped it!

Try this too!

You don't have to stick to these tasks. How about opening a food package, tying shoelaces, or writing a message? Can you think of any more?

THE TUBE CHALLENGE

Do you have the skills to pull off this amazing trick?

Play this on your own or with any number of others.

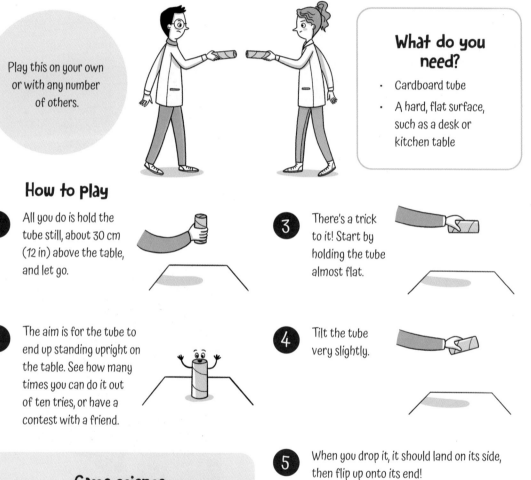

What do you need?

- Cardboard tube
- A hard, flat surface, such as a desk or kitchen table

How to play

1 All you do is hold the tube still, about 30 cm (12 in) above the table, and let go.

2 The aim is for the tube to end up standing upright on the table. See how many times you can do it out of ten tries, or have a contest with a friend.

3 There's a trick to it! Start by holding the tube almost flat.

4 Tilt the tube very slightly.

5 When you drop it, it should land on its side, then flip up onto its end!

Game science

The tube is slightly flexible and bouncy. If it lands on its end, it bounces and almost always falls over. But if it lands almost flat, the bounce will push it up into a standing position.

Ta-daaaa!

COIN MAGIC

Can you make the coin drop into the glass?
Yes, if you're quick enough!

What do you need?

- Playing card, postcard, or small piece of cardboard
- Coin
- Small glass or cup

Try this challenge alone or play against a friend.

How to play

1 Put the card on top of the glass, covering the opening, and put the coin in the middle on top.

2 Your challenge is to flick away the card so the coin falls into the glass. You can't pick the card up or bend it—just flick it.

3 The secret is to flick the card as hard as possible, making sure you flick it sideways, not up or down. This will make it shoot away, leaving the coin behind.

4 Once you've mastered it, try adding more coins on top of the first one. How many can you add?

Game science

This trick is all about friction, the force that slows or stops things when they rub together, and inertia, which makes objects keep doing what they're doing. The coin's inertia makes it stay still. If the card moves slowly, friction makes it grip the coin and the coin will move too. But if it's moving very fast, the friction isn't strong enough to take the coin with it, so it stays behind.

47

HOUSE OF CARDS

A house of cards is a tower or structure made from playing cards and nothing else—no glue or tape allowed! How high can you make it?

What do you need?

- One or more packs of playing cards
- A flat surface (you can use a table or desk, but some people find a carpet helps to grip the cards)

Try it on your own or compete with someone else.

How to play

 Build your tower by leaning cards against each other, laying more cards flat on top, then building higher. This is the most common method.

Aaarrggh!

2 Keep adding more cards! How high can you make your tower before it falls?

Is it harder or easier if you arrange the cards with the longest side at the bottom?

Game science

As there's nothing sticking the cards together, they are only held in place by gravity and friction. Where the cards touch, friction between them makes them grip onto each other. But it's not very strong, so you have to balance them very carefully. At some point, the weight of the cards will be too much, and gravity will pull the whole house of cards down.

CUP TOWER

Now for a slightly easier challenge: a tower of cups!

Challenge yourself, or have a contest with friends or family members.

How to play

1 If you have a lot of cups, you can build a pyramid-shaped tower and try to make it as high as possible.

What do you need?

- Paper cups
- A stopwatch (or phone stopwatch app)

2 If you don't have so many cups, you could build a small pyramid, but race to see who can do it the fastest.

3 Or try a different type of tower, like this one. How high can you make it?

Try this too!

Are there any other types of cup towers you could try? How about this?

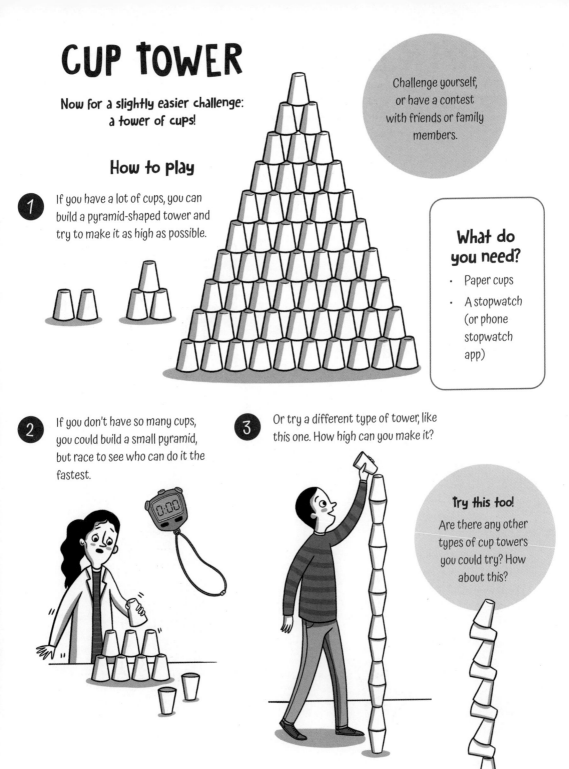

PAPER BRIDGE CHALLENGE

Designing bridges is an important job, as they have to carry heavy loads without falling down. Try it yourself with this paper bridge challenge.

Any number of players—you can build your own bridges or work as a team.

How to play

 1 Put the two chairs or tables about 30 cm (12 in) apart, creating a gap to bridge.

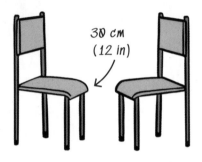

30 cm (12 in)

What do you need?

- Paper (it could be scrap paper, newspaper, old wrapping paper, or wallpaper)
- Two chairs or tables of the same height
- An unopened food can
- Scissors
- Tape
- String
- Extra materials such as paper straws, popsicle sticks, or pipe cleaners, if you have them (optional)

 2 Now start thinking about how to build a bridge. It has to cross the gap, touching only the two sides (not the floor in between). When it's finished, it must be strong enough to hold the food can without breaking or tipping the can off.

You can sketch your ideas first, if you like.

Here are a few tips:
Rolling paper into a tube makes it much stronger.

You could look on the internet for photos of famous bridges ...

So does folding it into a zigzag.

.... and look at real bridges the next time you are out!

Use several layers of paper together if one isn't thick enough.

3 When you're ready, start building, then test your bridge with the food can.

Try this too!

For a tougher challenge, see if you can build a bridge using ONLY paper—nothing else! You'll have to use rolling, folding, and wrapping to hold it together and make it strong enough.

Game science

A good bridge will not bend or break when there's a weight pushing it down in the middle. You can do this by making sure it's very strong and rigid. Or you can use some kind of string or support to hold the bridge up. This is how a suspension bridge works—it has towers with cables attached that the bridge hangs from.

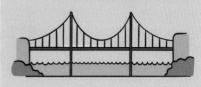

DOMINO RUN

As you know, if you knock over one domino, all the others fall down.
(If you've set them up right!) What's the longest domino run you can make?

How to play

1 To make a domino run, stand the dominoes on their ends in a row. They must be close enough together so that when each domino falls, it pushes the next one over.

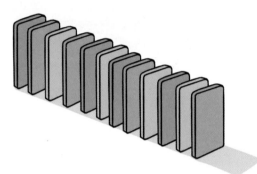

2 When you're finished, push over the first domino and watch them go!

3 You can try other things too:

What do you need?

- A clear, flat space on a table or on the floor.
- Dominoes!*

*You can use a traditional set of dominoes, or several sets, if possible. You might be able to borrow extra sets from friends and family, and you can often buy dominoes very cheaply at thrift stores or charity shops. You can also buy larger packs of special toppling dominoes at toy stores.

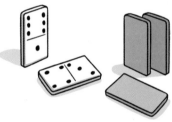

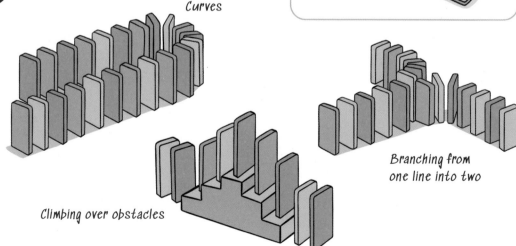

Curves

Climbing over obstacles

Branching from one line into two

4 And if you have lots of dominoes, try to make the longest run you can.

Handy tip!

When you're setting up a long run, leave a gap every so often. If you accidentally knock a domino down before you've finished, only a few will fall over.

Game science

Why do dominoes topple so easily? It's because their tall, narrow shape means they're not very stable. It only takes a slight push to knock a domino down, so when one falls, the whole row goes too.

If you put the dominoes like this, it wouldn't work at all.

What about this? Try it and see if it works.

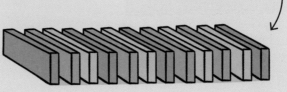

EXTENDING ARM GRABBER

Do you ever wish you could reach something that's a little too far away?
Maybe this grabber is the answer!

What do you need?

- Corrugated cardboard—an old packing box is perfect
- Ruler
- Marker pen
- Scissors
- Skewer or large needle
- Split pins or cocktail sticks

This is easy to do on your own or as a group, or you could have a contest to see who can make the longest working grabber.

How to play

1 Mark and cut out six rectangles from a piece of cardboard. Each one should be about 2.5 cm (1 in) wide and 15 cm (6 in) long. Line them up the same way as the ridges in the corrugated cardboard, as this will make them stronger.

15 cm (6 in)

2.5 cm (1 in)

2 On another piece of cardboard, draw and cut out two more rectangles the same size, but give them grabber ends.

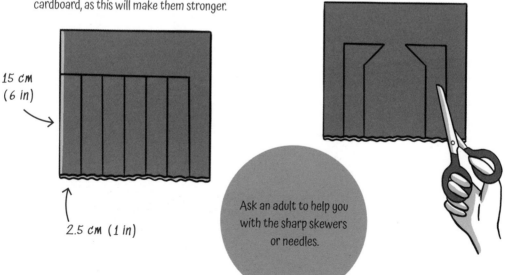

Ask an adult to help you with the sharp skewers or needles.

3 With an adult's help, use the skewer or needle to make holes in the middle and ends of all the pieces, like this.

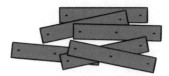

4 Now you can fit the pieces together by sticking split pins or short sections of cocktail stick through the holes. First, join the pairs of pieces in a crisscross shape.

5 Then join the crisscrosses together.

6 Use the grabber pieces to make the last section.

7 Hold the other end of your grabber and open and close it to make it work.

Game science

The grabber passes your movements from one end to the other, as each section makes the next section move in the same way. You couldn't make it reeeeeeallly long, as eventually it would get too heavy and bend or break. But you could probably make it longer than this. Try it and see!

What can you pick up?

EGG DROP CHALLENGE

For your next challenge, you have to drop an egg on the ground. Sounds easy, right? But wait! You also have to make sure it doesn't break!

Any number of people can play, as long as there's one egg per person!

Heeeelp!

What do you need?

· A fresh, raw egg for each person (no boiled eggs—that's cheating!)

· A chair or low wall to stand on to drop the eggs

· A plastic sheet to put on the ground to catch any mess

· A range of craft materials, such as:

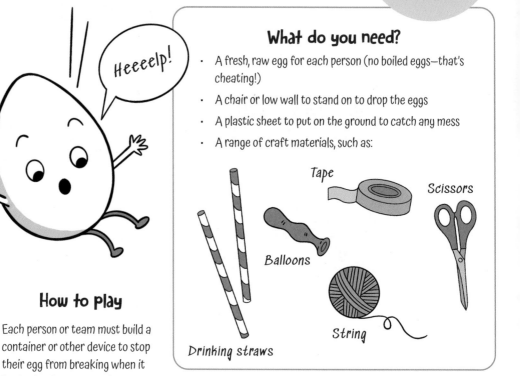

Tape

Scissors

Balloons

String

Drinking straws

How to play

1 Each person or team must build a container or other device to stop their egg from breaking when it lands. Here's one example:

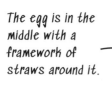

The egg is in the middle with a framework of straws around it.

When it lands, the straws should take the impact, making sure the egg doesn't smash into the ground and crack.

But will it work? Or will the straws crumple too quickly, leading to a messy EGG-splosion?

2 Egg-speriment with different methods and materials to give your egg a soft landing. Then, when everyone's ready, test out your designs! Ask an adult to drop each one from the exact same height—and see if the eggs survive!

Test out some alternative designs!

Game science

An egg breaks when you drop it because it speeds up as it falls, hitting the ground hard and breaking its thin shell. There are two main ways to protect it:

· Cushion it by surrounding it with something to slow it down when it lands.

· Make it fall slowly, using some kind of parachute or wing.

(Or try a combination of both!)

RAFT CHALLENGE

If you're ever stuck on a desert island, building a raft could come in handy ... why not try it in miniature?

How to play

 1 Put some water in your bathtub or inflatable pool until it's about 10 cm (4 in) deep. You can use it while you build your raft to check which things float best.

 2 Now start experimenting and designing your raft. It needs parts that will make it float, and a flat deck for your toy figures to stand or sit on. It should also be quite wide and flat, so that it can't tip over.

Fun for any number of people.

What do you need?

- A bathtub or inflatable pool
- Scissors
- Toy figures to ride on the rafts
- Raft-building materials, such as:

  Twigs, popsicle sticks, or cocktail sticks

  Corks

  String

  Rubber bands

  Small bottles, tubes, or waterproof containers with lids, such as vitamin bottles

  Straws

  Polystyrene packaging

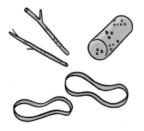

Empty, sealed bottles, corks, or polystyrene are good at floating.

Sticks or straws could make a good flat deck.

Make sure an adult is there to supervise when you're using the bathtub or inflatable pool.

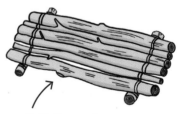

Hold the parts together with string or rubber bands.

3 When your raft is ready, try sailing it on the water with some little people on board. Let's hope they don't fall in!

Free at last!

Try this too!

A catamaran is a type of boat with two separate floating parts joined together, making it more stable. Could you build a raft that works like this?

Game science

Like the other floating things in this book, corks, empty bottles, and polystyrene float because they are lighter for their size, or less dense, than water. However, when you add the deck, the string or rubber bands to hold the raft together, and the crew, it will get denser. You have to balance adding all the parts you need with keeping the raft light enough to float.

CARDBOARD CHAIR CHALLENGE

For this challenge, you have to make a chair or stool that you can actually sit on out of cardboard. If it works, you'll have a new chair too.

How to play

 First, you need to figure out how big to make your chair. Look at other chairs to find the best height and the size for the seat to be.

You can do this on your own, but working as a team can help you come up with good ideas.

What do you need?

- Large pieces of corrugated cardboard or old packing boxes.
- Ruler
- Marker pen
- Scissors
- Tape
- Glue

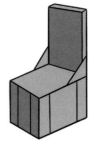

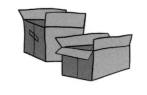 Now think about the design of your chair. It will need a flat seat and a strong part underneath to hold the seat up. Most chairs have legs, but if you made thin legs out of cardboard, would they be strong enough?

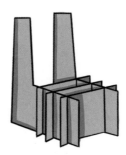

Do you want to add a back, or will your chair be a simple stool?

3 Experiment with using the cardboard in different ways—fold it, roll it, tape it, or glue it to make different shapes. See what ideas you come up with.

4 When you're ready, construct your chair, then test it out by sitting on it. Be careful!

Cardboard can sometimes seem quite weak, but use it in the right way and it's easily strong enough to support you. For example:

• The ridges or lines in the cardboard give it extra strength. When they are vertical (running straight up and down), the cardboard is much stronger.

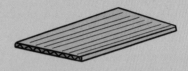

• You can also make corrugated cardboard stronger by sticking two flat sheets together, with the ridges running in different directions.

• Triangles are strong, because the three sides hold each other in a fixed position. If you fold cardboard into triangle shapes, it will hold more weight.

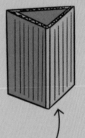

A shape like this could make a strong chair leg.

• Rolling cardboard into tubes also creates a strong structure.

GIANT BUBBLES

What's more fun than bubbles? Ginormous bubbles!

What do you need?

- Large plastic bowl or pail
- 2.5 l (11 cups) warm water
- 1 l (4 cups) dish soap
- 125 ml (0.5 cup) glycerine (from a hobby store or supermarket)

- Two thin bamboo poles or garden sticks
- Thin string
- Scissors
- Tape measure
- A safe outdoor space

How to play

1 Put the bowl or pail outdoors and add the water, dish soap, and glycerine. Stir the mixture slowly, so it doesn't bubble up, and set it aside.

2 To make the giant bubble wand, cut two pieces of string: one 1 m (39 in) long and one 1.2 m (47 in) long.

Tie the ends of the shorter string to the ends of your two sticks.

Tie the ends of the longer string to the shorter string, close to the sticks. (You might need an adult to help you tie tight, strong knots.)

3 Now for your bubbles! Hold the other ends of the sticks and lower the strings into the bubble mixture. Then slowly lift them out again, and hold them wide apart to stretch out the string.

4 Lift the bubble wand up high to catch the wind, and it should blow a giant bubble! Or, if there's no wind, sweep the wand through the air.

NET BUBBLES

Instead of a big bubble, make lots of little ones with a net wand.

What do you need?

- A bubble wand like the one opposite
- Extra string
- Scissors

How to play

1 Cut eight pieces of string, each 1.2 m (47 in) long. Tie them along the top string of your bubble wand so they're evenly spaced.

2 Tie each string in the middle, leaving the two long ends hanging down.

3 Then tie each string to the next string along, about 10 cm (4 in) down from the top.

4 Keep doing this until you get to the other string on the wand, and tie the net strings to it.

Try using your net as a bubble wand, and see what happens!

Game science

Soap contains special molecules. One end sticks to water, and the other end pushes it away.

When you mix soap and water, this creates layers of water with soap on both sides.

A layer like this can stretch out into a thin film or sheet and make a bubble.

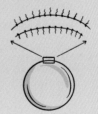

SPAGHETTI SKYSCRAPERS

Try the ultimate classic science game and see how tall you can make a tower of spaghetti.

Before doing this, make sure no one is allergic to the ingredients in the spaghetti or marshmallows. If they are, you may be able to use alternatives.

How to play

Try it on your own or compete against friends or family.

 1 Stick the ends of the spaghetti into the marshmallows to hold them together. How tall can you make your tower?

You can make shapes like squares, triangles, boxes, and crisscross shapes ...

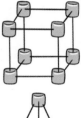

... and join them together to make towers or other buildings.

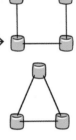

What do you need?

- Packet of dried spaghetti
- Large package of medium-sized marshmallows
- A flat, firm surface to build on

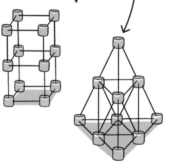

Experiment with different methods and designs, and see how high you can build.

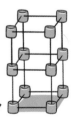

Game science

Building spaghetti skyscrapers uses a lot of the same methods as real skyscrapers! For example:

- You need to balance strength with lightness, so your tower can be tall without falling down.
- Triangles are very strong shapes, so using them to build will help your tower stay up.
- Making your whole tower triangle-shaped is a good way to make it as tall and light as possible.
- You can make the base extra strong by using two spaghetti sticks at a time ... but near the top, use single sticks.

QUAKEPROOF TOWERS

Using the same spaghetti building method, try a different challenge ...

How to play

 1 Each person should build their spaghetti structure on a cutting board or tray.

 2 This time, instead of the tallest tower, you're aiming for a strong building that will withstand an earthquake. Decide on a maximum height, such as 30 cm (12 in) and try to make your building as sturdy and indestructible as possible.

 3 Squish the marshmallows at the bottom down to help them stick to the board or tray.

4 Then test your building by holding the sides of the board or tray on a flat surface, and give it a good shake!

What do you need?

· Spaghetti and marshmallows
· Large trays or cutting boards

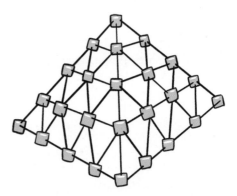

Push it quickly to and fro.

How well did your design hold up?

STROOP SCIENCE

For this game, all you have to do is try not to read! Sounds easy, right?

How to play

 To create your Stroop board, grab some bright pens or pencils and start writing the names of different shades ... in the wrong shade! For example, you might write the word "blue" in red, or "orange" in green.

 Try reading out the words. Pretty easy, huh? Set the timer and see how quickly you can read them all.

 Now, do it again, but this time, don't say the word. Instead, say whether the word is red, blue, green, yellow, orange, and so on. As they don't match, you have to try not to read the word, and instead just look at it.

> Orange, blue, green ...

 Ask the other person to set the timer, and ... go! How long did it take this time?

Who did it the quickest?

What do you need?

- Timer or stopwatch
- Piece of paper
- Pens or pencils in different shades

Game science

This strange science game is known as the Stroop Effect (named after scientist John Ridley Stroop). Most people find part two is much harder than part one, and it takes much longer. That's because, once we learn to read, we automatically read words as soon as we see them. The information zooms straight into your brain before you think about anything else. When you're trying not to read, but looking for other information instead, your brain still can't help reading, so it gets confused and slows down.

SHAPE STROOP

Here's another Stroop-style game to try, using shapes and shape words.

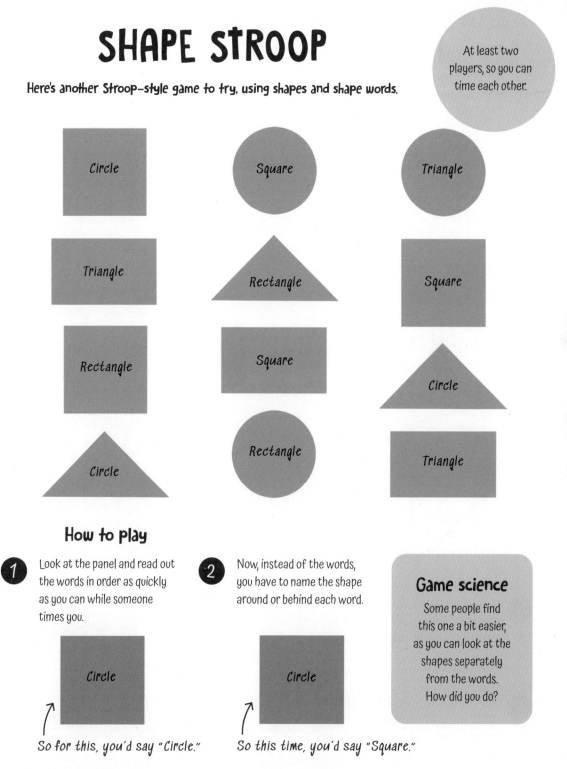

Circle

Square

Triangle

Triangle

Rectangle

Square

Rectangle

Square

Circle

Circle

Rectangle

Triangle

How to play

1 Look at the panel and read out the words in order as quickly as you can while someone times you.

Circle

So for this, you'd say "Circle."

2 Now, instead of the words, you have to name the shape around or behind each word.

Circle

So this time, you'd say "Square."

Game science

Some people find this one a bit easier, as you can look at the shapes separately from the words. How did you do?

MIRROR MASTERPIECE

What happens if you try to draw a picture in the mirror?

This is easy to do on your own, but it's even more fun watching other people try!

What do you need?

- Mirror with a stand
- Cereal box or similar-sized box
- Pen and paper
- Table and chair

Make sure an adult is there when you're moving mirrors around.

How to play

1 Sit at the table and stand the mirror in front of you, about 30 cm (12 in) away. Put a piece of paper on the table in front of it.

2 Stand the cereal box in between you and the paper, so you can see the paper reflected in the mirror, but not in real life.

3 Now, reach around the cereal box with the pen, and start drawing on the paper. You can only see what you're doing by looking in the mirror.

4 Try to draw a simple picture.

5 If you're playing with other people, you could think of something to draw and see if they can guess what it is.

Game science

As you've probably discovered, this is not easy. It may feel as if your brain has completely forgotten how to control your hands! That's because your brain is used to seeing your hands move in a particular way when it sends them instructions. In a mirror, where they go is reversed. It's really hard for your brain to get used to that, so it keeps sending the wrong instructions. However, if you keep trying, your brain will get used to it, and it will get easier.

MIRROR MESSAGE

Here's another game to try in the mirror—writing a message!

How to play

1 This time, think of a word or message and see if you can write it clearly enough to read. Or ask other people to try to guess what it is as you're writing.

What do you need?

- Set up your mirror, paper, and pen just like in the game opposite.

I WENT TO THE MARKET

This memory game is easy at first, but it gets harder and harder ...

This is a game for two or more players.

What do you need?

- Nothing—just your memory!

How to play

1 Choose one person to go first, then take turns. The first player says:

I went to the market, and I bought ...

... then names an item from the market, such as a loaf of bread.

2 The next player says:

I went to the market and I bought a loaf of bread, and ...

... then adds another item, such as a bag of apples.

3 Then keep going! On each turn, you have to remember the previous items in the right order, and add your own.

I went to the market and I bought a loaf of bread, a bag of apples, some grapes, a box of eggs, some teabags and ...

Game science

How soon did you start forgetting things? We store thousands of words, objects, and other things in our permanent, long-term memory. But the brain's short-term memory can only hold about six or seven things at once before we start forgetting them.

MAZE MEMORY

How does your brain remember the right way to go?

How to play

1 Set the timer, and start solving the maze. (Don't draw on the book, just use your finger to find the right route.)

2 As soon as you finish it, stop the timer and write down how long you took.

3 Then do it again! And then a few more times. Each time you complete the maze, write down how long it took.

What do you need?

- A stopwatch or timer
- Pen and paper
- The maze on this page

Do this on your own, or play with a friend and take turns timing each other.

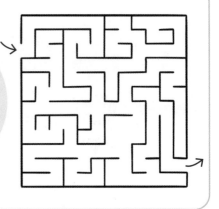

Game science

You should find that as you do the maze over and over again, you get faster. Your brain starts storing knowledge about the right route and remembers it for next time.

This is how we learn other things too, like the way to school, playing the piano, or tying shoelaces. As you learn, your brain cells make new connections, changing and growing to store new information. The more you try, the stronger the memory gets, until doing the task starts to feel automatic.

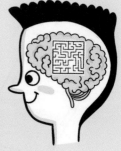

"TRAIN" A FRIEND!

Animals such as dogs can't speak our language, yet we can teach them to behave in particular ways. How do they know what we want them to do? Try this and see!

What do you need?

- Buttons, counters, or small coins to use as "treats"
- A room with lots of things in it

This is for two or more players.

How to play

1 Choose one person to be the "dog", and ask them to leave the room. While they're out, decide what it is that you want to teach them to do. It could be something like opening a book, turning a lamp on, or picking up a particular pen.

2 Now bring the "dog" back in and ask them to stand in the middle of the room. Tell them they'll get treats for doing the right thing, and they need to collect as many treats as possible. All they have to do is start doing things around the room.

3 Each time they get closer to doing what you want, give them a treat!

For example, suppose you want them to open a book. Give them a treat when ...

- They move toward the bookshelf
- They look at the bookshelf
- They touch a book
- They take a book out

 4 When they finally open a book, give them another treat and lots of praise.

Good dog!

Well done!

What a clever boy!

What a good girl!

5 But when they do something that has nothing to do with the task, don't do anything. Don't say "no"—just stay quiet.

Game science

Even though the "dog" has no idea what you want them to do, this training method can train them to do it. It's called positive reinforcement. Whenever they do something right, they get a treat. That makes them feel good, and it becomes a thing they want to keep doing. Real dogs are exactly the same!

WHAT'S THAT SMELL?

Can you trust your brain to tell you what you can smell? Not always!

Try it on your own or amaze your friends!

Is my brain lying to me?

What do you need?

- Three cups or glasses
- Cocoa powder
- Ground cinnamon
- Teaspoons
- A timer

How to play

1 Put two teaspoonfuls of cocoa powder into one cup and two teaspoonfuls of cinnamon into another. In the third cup, mix a teaspoon of cocoa powder and a teaspoon of cinnamon together.

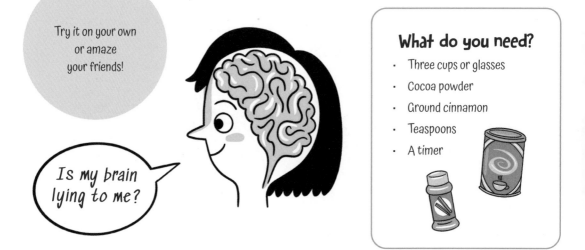

↑ Cocoa powder   ↑ Cinnamon   ↑ A mixture of both

2 Now set the timer for 30 seconds and start sniffing the cocoa powder. Keep smelling it until the timer goes off.

Mmmmm, chocolatey ...

3 As soon as the 30 seconds are up, quickly switch to the cup with the mixture in it and smell that. What does it smell like?

4 Then try it the other way around. Sniff the cinnamon for 30 seconds, then smell the mixture. What does it smell like this time?

That's weird!

Game science

You should find the mixture smells totally different, depending on what you've just been sniffing! If you've been sniffing the cocoa powder, the mixture will smell like cinnamon. And if you've been sniffing the cinnamon, it will smell like cocoa powder!

That's because when your brain keeps getting the same signal over and over, it starts to ignore it so you don't notice it so much. So, when you've been smelling cocoa powder for 30 seconds, you become less sensitive to it. The mixture smells more of cinnamon, because your brain hasn't got used to that and notices it more.

This also happens when there's a funny smell in a room, or a background noise. Your brain starts to tune them out so that you stop noticing them.

Same mixture ... different smells!

Try this too!

To play with friends, don't tell them what's in the cup containing the mixture and see if they can guess.

TASTING BLUE

Does it matter what food looks like?
Test it with this simple game.

You need at least one other person to do the test on, as well as an adult to help you prepare.

What do you need?

- White or pale food or foods, such as rice pudding, white pasta, or mashed potato
- Blue food dye
- Two plates and two forks or spoons

As this involves cooking or preparing food, you'll need an adult to help. Also, make sure beforehand that no one is allergic to any of the food you're using.

How to play

1 With an adult helper, prepare your food. For example, you could cook some white pasta, cook some potatoes and mash them, make some instant mashed potatoes, or open a container of rice pudding.

2 Put half the food on one of the plates. Add a few drops of blue food dye to the other half and stir it in well. When it's a nice bright blue, put it on the other plate.

3 Dinner is served! Ask your test subject to come and try the food. Show them the two plates, and tell them that both are exactly the same, but you've dyed one blue.

4 Ask them which they think looks best, and which they'd prefer to eat. Ask them to try both. Do they want to? Do they like one more than the other?

Game science

Even if people know that the bright blue food will taste normal, they are likely to say "ewww!" or not want to try it. Scientists think this is because blue foods are rare in nature. But decaying food can look blue, so we associate it with food that's gone bad.

However, blue candy or chewing gum is not so off-putting. You're used to them containing artificial dyes, and don't find it so weird.

Urgh, gross!

THREE LITTLE BOXES

How can three boxes be lighter than one of them on its own?
They can't—but this science game can make it feel as if they are.

What do you need?

- Three small, flat, identical boxes, such as empty matchboxes or small storage containers (They must not be transparent.)
- Coins, small pebbles, or other small, heavy objects, enough to fill one box

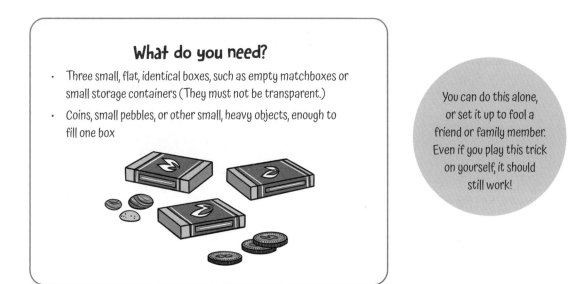

You can do this alone, or set it up to fool a friend or family member. Even if you play this trick on yourself, it should still work!

How to play

1 Fill one of the boxes with the coins, pebbles, or other objects, so that it's a lot heavier than the other two, and close it.

2 Stack the two empty boxes together, then put the third, heavier box on top.

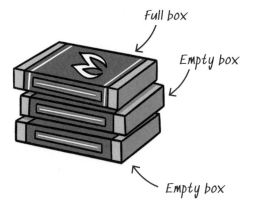

Full box

Empty box

Empty box

3 Now pick up the top box and feel how heavy it is. Or, if you're testing someone else, ask them to do it.

4 Now put the box back and lift up all three boxes together. How heavy do they feel now?

Game science

Amazingly, most people find that the three boxes together feel lighter than the single heavy box on its own! This happens even though we all know it's not possible to make something lighter by adding more objects to it.

Scientists are still not sure exactly why this happens, and what's going on in our brains to give us the wrong information. It could be that lifting the heavy box first gives you an idea of what each box should weigh. So you expect the stack of three boxes to be about three times heavier than the first one. Instead, it feels unexpectedly light and your brain interprets this as being even lighter than it really is.

THE SPEED OF MUSIC

Time for some music! But beware—it could do strange things to your brain ...

How to play

1 Ask the other person or people to sit and listen, and give them each a pencil and paper.

2 Tell them you're going to play them some music, and they have to guess how long it was playing. Play the faster piece of music, timing it for exactly 40 seconds (make sure only you can see the timer). Afterwards, ask them to write down how long they think it lasted.

3 Now do the same with the slow music, again for 40 seconds. Then ask them to write down how long they think that lasted.

4 Now have a look at the results! Each test lasted 40 seconds, but only you know that. Did people think time went by faster or slower during the different tests?

What do you need?

- Something to play music on, such as a phone or computer
- Two different songs or pieces of music: one fast and exciting, one slow and peaceful
- Stopwatch or timer
- Pencil and paper

You need at least one other person to do the test on, and an adult to help you with the music.

Game science

Scientists have found that slower or faster music can change how fast you think time is passing. Faster music often makes people think more time has gone by—maybe because more sounds and beats have been fitted in. However, people are less likely to get it wrong if they are musicians themselves.

Thud!

GUESS THE SOUND

Tinkle!

this is a quick and easy sound science game!

How to play

1 Write a list of the objects and give it to the other person. Ask them to face away from you while you put one object at a time into the container, then shake it and turn it over to make a sound. They have to guess which object it is.

This game is for at least two players.

How did they do?

What do you need?

- Non-transparent container with a lid, such as a coffee can
- Pen and paper
- Small objects, such as:

  Coin

  Cork

  Eraser

  Key

  Marble

  Buttons

  Pebble

  Rubber band

Game science

Sounds are made when moving things vibrate, or jiggle to and fro, and make the air around them vibrate too. Different objects and materials vibrate in different ways, and that's why they sound different—and our brains get used to spotting these differences. Your guesser might not get them all right, but they can probably make a good guess.

SKELETON BINGO

You might be familiar with the game of beetle bingo ...
but this time, let's draw a skeleton.

For at least
two players.

What do you need?

- A pen and pencil for each player
- A picture of the skeleton, shown on the right, to copy
- Dice

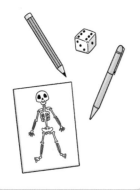

How to set up

1 All the players sit around a table and take turns to throw the dice. When it's your turn, roll the dice once. The number you roll will decide what part of the skeleton you can draw on your paper.

1 = Body

4 = An arm

2 = Head

5 = A hand

3 = A leg

6 = A foot

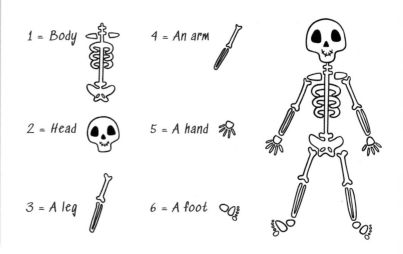

2 However, you can't get started on your skeleton until you roll a 1, as you have to draw the body before you can add the head, arms, or legs. And you can't add hands or feet until you have arms or legs to add them to.

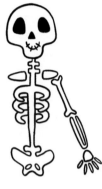

3 If you roll a number you can't use, you have to wait until it's your turn again. For example, you might roll a 6 for a foot, but if you don't have a leg to put it on, you can't draw anything.

Arrrgh!

4 The first person to complete their skeleton is the winner!

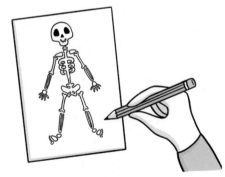

(And now everyone will know how to draw skeletons, too.)

Game science

Humans and many other animals share the same basic body plan: a torso or main body with a backbone and ribs, a head, and four limbs. If you look at pictures of skeletons of birds, lizards, frogs, cats, dogs, horses, and even dinosaurs, you'll see the same pattern. See if you can match their skeleton parts to the parts of a human skeleton. Do they have any extra or different parts?

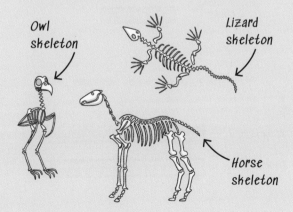

Owl skeleton

Lizard skeleton

Horse skeleton

DNA PAIRS

Build a strand of DNA by matching the right pairs together—just like real DNA does!

What is DNA?

DNA is found inside living cells. It's a chemical that forms a twisted ladder shape, with rungs made up of four different parts called bases.

The pattern of bases acts as a code, containing instructions that control how cells work.

This game is for two or more players.

The bases are called Adenine, Cytosine, Guanine, and Thymine—or A, C, G, and T for short.

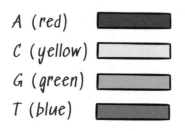

A (red)
C (yellow)
G (green)
T (blue)

They always match up in the same pairs:

A with T
C with G

What do you need?

- Red, yellow, green, and blue paper or cardboard (or white cardboard and red, yellow, green, and blue marker pens)
- Scissors
- Stopwatch or timer

How to play

 Cut out lots of finger-sized strips of cardboard to make bases, making sure you have at least ten red, ten yellow, ten green, and ten blue.

Did you know?

DNA is short for Deoxyribonucleic Acid.

 One player should then make half a DNA strand by making a row of ten bases, like this. You can use any combination in any order.

3 The other person has to add the right bases to make matching pairs, as fast as possible—remembering that A (red) always goes with T (blue), and C (yellow) always goes with G (green).

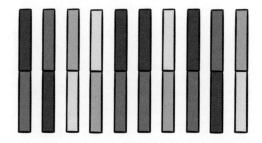

4 Use the timer to see how long it takes them, then swap places and set up a different pattern.

Game science

Inside a real cell, DNA does this when it needs to make a copy of itself, so that a cell can divide into two new cells. The DNA ladder splits down the middle, and new bases join onto the two halves to make two new strands of DNA. Then each new cell can have its own copy. Genius!

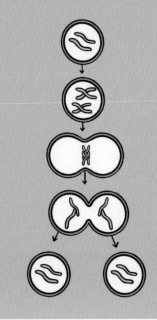

RAINBOW WHEEL

The ultimate simple science toy, this is easy to make in just a few minutes.

How to play

1 Draw around your round object on the card, and cut out the circle.

What do you need?

- White card
- A round object to draw around, about 7–10 cm (3–4 in) across, such as a bowl
- Pencil
- Scissors
- Ruler
- Marker pens in red, orange, yellow, green, blue, and purple

2 Draw three lines across the middle of the circle to make six sections. (It doesn't matter if they're not exactly equal, but make them as equal as you can.)

3 Fill in the six sections in red, orange, yellow, green, blue, and purple, in that order.

Game science

If you spin it fast enough, you should see something mindboggling—the circle turns white! But why?

Light travels in waves. The waves can have different lengths. Blue light, for example, has shorter waves than red light. When we see white light, we're looking at all the wavelengths mixed together.

The spinning circle mixes up the wavelengths so we seem them all together, which makes it look white.

4 Stick your pencil down through the middle of the circle. (If this is too difficult, ask an adult to help you make a hole first.)

Now spin the wheel like a spinning top and see what happens!

BALANCING BUTTERFLY

Make a butterfly that can mysteriously balance on its head.

For any number of people.

What do you need?

- Cardboard (quite firm, not too thin and bendy)
- Marker pens
- Scissors
- Pencil
- Two small coins
- Tape

How to play

 1 Draw a butterfly shape like the one below onto cardboard. The top of the wingtips must be higher than the top of the head.

2 Decorate your butterfly, then carefully cut it out with scissors.

3 Turn the butterfly over and tape the two small coins to the tips of its upper wings.

 4 You should now be able to balance the butterfly on your finger—or on a pencil, or even on your nose.

How are you doing that!?

Game science

The butterfly balances because the coins make the tips of the wings heavier. They reach out past its head and balance out the rest of the butterfly, even though it looks much bigger.

Because of the weights, the butterfly balances here, not in the middle.

JUMPING BEANS

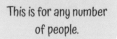

Real jumping beans, found in Mexico, have tiny baby insects living inside them, which make them jump and jiggle around. But don't worry, this homemade version doesn't contain any bugs!

This is for any number of people.

How to play

1 Cut a piece of foil about 6 cm (2 in) wide and 8 cm (3 in) long. Gently press and smooth it flat on a hard surface, like a tabletop.

2 Roll the foil around your cylinder-shaped object. Then slide the object out of the foil, to leave a tube.

3 Put a marble into the foil tube, then fold and pinch the ends closed (it doesn't matter if they're a bit messy).

4 Now put the tube with the marble inside into a food container, put the lid on, and shake the food container for about ten seconds. The marble will shape the ends and make them smooth and curved, creating a bean shape.

5 Now your jumping bean is ready! Roll it across your hands or down a gentle slope to make it flip and jump.

What do you need?

- Kitchen foil or a foil chocolate wrapper
- Marbles
- Scissors
- A cylinder-shaped object slightly wider than your marbles, such as a lip balm tube or large marker
- A food container with a lid

Help!

Game science

The bean moves in a strange way because the marble is free to roll around inside it. On a slope, the marble rolls down inside the bean, hits the end, and makes it flip over.

CONSTELLATION CASTERS

Constellations are patterns of stars in the night sky, which we give names to based on what they look like. With this activity, you can create some amazing constellations on your bedroom wall.

How to play

1 Draw around a round object onto the piece of cardboard to make circles, and cut them out.

2 For each card circle, choose a constellation you like, and carefully copy it onto the card. Draw dots for the stars and connect them with lines. You can add the name of the constellation, too.

Any number of players.

What do you need?

- Cardboard (cereal boxes or other food boxes will work well)
- A round object to draw around, about 10 cm (4 in) across
- Pencil
- Scissors
- A skewer, cocktail stick, or thick needle
- Pictures of constellations, in a book or on the internet
- Flashlight

3 With an adult to help, use the skewer, cocktail stick, or needle to make holes through all the star dots.

4 Now you can light up your constellations! In a dark room, hold each card in front of a flashlight and shine the light onto a wall. Can you recognize the constellations without the lines joining the stars together?

Game science

Constellations look like patterns, but the stars are really just randomly scattered. The stars in a constellation are often not close to each other at all—some are much farther away than others. But the human brain always looks for familiar shapes in random patterns, so we see pictures and shapes in the stars.

AIR BLASTER

Make your own air blaster,
also known as a vortex cannon.

Ask an adult to help
when you're using
sharp objects
like skewers.

How to play

1 Ask an adult to help you cut the bottom end off your bottle with the sharp scissors.

2 Cut the neck off the balloon and stretch the other part of the balloon over the bottom end of the bottle. Leave the middle of the balloon slightly loose so that you can grab it.

3 Use tape to hold the balloon on firmly.

4 Your blaster is ready to use! To make a blast of air, pull and stretch the balloon toward you, then let it go. The air will shoot out of the bottle neck and hit whatever's in the way.

What do you need?

- Small plastic drinks bottle
- Balloon
- Strong, sharp scissors
- Tape
- Objects to aim at, such as dominoes or cardboard tubes

Game science

As you pull back the balloon, the blaster sucks in extra air. Then, when you let go, the air inside is forced through the narrow bottle neck, shooting out at high speed!

Try this too!

If you don't have a bottle, you can make an air cannon with a large paper cup. Cut a small hole about 4 cm (1.5 in) across out of the base of the cup, and put the balloon over the other end.

CONFETTI POPPER

A super-simple popper to fill the air with confetti!

What do you need?

- Clean, dry cardboard toilet paper tube
- Balloon
- Ruler
- Scissors
- Tape
- Confetti, or little pieces of cut-up newspaper, wrapping paper, or old cards

How to play

1 Tie the neck of the balloon closed (without blowing it up first!), then cut the balloon in half across the middle,.

2 Stretch the tied end of the balloon over one end of the tube and hold it in place with tape.

3 Put a handful of confetti in your popper, pull the balloon down, aim, and fire!

Pop!

The game science for this page is the same as page 90.

PAPER PLANE LAUNCHER

This launcher uses an rubber band to store up energy. When it's released, it springs back and pushes the plane forward!

For any number of people—just make one each!

How to play

1 Make a few basic paper darts. First, fold a piece of paper in half lengthways, then open it out again.

2 Fold the corners into the middle at one end.

What do you need?

- Paper and stapler
- A piece of thin cardboard roughly the same size as the paper
- Large rubber band, about 15–18 cm (6–7 in) long

3 Then fold the sides in again to meet the middle.

4 Fold the dart in half and fold down the sides to make flat wings.

5 To make the launcher, fold your cardboard in half widthways.

6 Fold the two sides in half again.

7 And then fold the side flaps in half again.

8 Staple a rubber band here.

8 Loop your rubber band over the launcher, like this.

Then place a paper dart in the fold inside the rubber band.

9 Point the launcher away from you.

To launch the dart, gently pull apart the flaps at the end nearest you.

AMAZING RING WING

It's a tube of paper, but it flies like a plane!

What do you need?

- A piece of paper
- Tape
- A cylinder-shaped object, such as a jar or bottle

How to play

1 Fold one of the longest edges of the paper in thirds.

2 Press it down and press along the fold to make it crisp.

3 Fold the folded section in half, pressing it down firmly, then fold the folded section in half again.

4 Now wrap your paper strip around the cylinder-shaped object with the fold inward to make it curved.

5 Curl it into a tube, fitting one end of the folded part inside the other, and use tape to hold it together.

6 It's ready! To fly it, hold the ring wing up in the air with the folded end at the front, and tilt it very slightly upward. Then give it a good push and let go.

Game science

As the wing flies forward, air flows through it and around it and is pushed slightly downward, which in turn pushes the wing up and helps it stay in the air.

TIGHTROPE BALANCER

Can you balance a cork on a tightrope made of string? Yes, if you know how ...

Ask an adult to supervise when you're using sharp skewers or kebab sticks, and to help you tie the string.

Challenge a friend, then show them how it's done.

What do you need?

- A cork, or a medium sized eraser will work well too
- String
- Two kebab sticks or skewers
- Sticky putty, craft clay, or small erasers

How to play

 Ask an adult to help you tie a piece of string between two fixed objects, such as coat hooks, window locks, or stair banisters. (Don't use furniture, as it could move or pull over.) The string can be flat or slightly sloping.

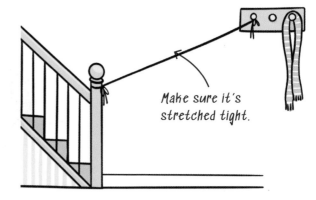

Make sure it's stretched tight.

2 Now challenge a friend or family member to balance the cork or eraser on the string, like a tightrope walker. Can they do it? (Bet they can't!)

 **3** But you can! Stick your two skewers into the sides of the cork or eraser, sloping downward. Then add small weights to the ends, such as balls of sticky putty or small erasers.

Try balancing it again!

Game science

You've made the cork or eraser heavier, yet it balances easier! This is because the skewers and weights make the tightrope balancer heavier below the level of the tightrope. It can't tip off, because the weight below the string pulls it into an upright position. You could try making it wobble to and fro, though.

Whoo-ooo-aaah!

Try this too!

Make your tightrope balancer a little paper outfit and head if you like!

That's better! I can see!

CASTLE DESTROYER

Long ago, armies used giant catapults to knock down enemy castles. Try doing the same with this mini version!

Build your own or compete with friends to see who can knock down the other's castle first.

You'll never destroy Box Castle!

Watch me!

Make sure there's an adult around when you're using this, and don't fire your catapult at people, animals, or anything breakable!

What do you need?

- Nine wooden frozen dessert sticks or craft sticks
- Six rubber bands
- A strong plastic, wooden, or metal teaspoon
- Craft clay, small erasers, or kitchen foil to make missiles
- Small, light cardboard boxes
- Tape

How to play

1 Take seven sticks, stack them up, and attach the ends together with two rubber bands.

2 Stack the remaining two sticks together and loop a rubber band tightly around one end.

3 Fit the stack of seven sticks in between the two sticks.

4 Loop a rubber band several times around all the sticks where they cross over, to hold them firmly in place.

5 Finally, use two rubber bands to attach the spoon to the top stick.

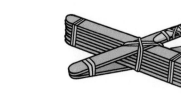

6 Use your boxes to build a simple castle or castle wall.

7 Prepare some missiles. You can use small erasers, balls of soft craft clay, or cannonballs made from tightly rolled up foil.

8 To use your catapult, place a missile on the spoon, hold the catapult steady, pull the spoon down, then let go.

Game science

When you pull down the spoon, it stretches the rubber bands and also slightly bends the springy wooden stick. When you let go, they spring back, pushing the spoon up. The spoon soon stops as it's attached to the catapult, but the missile flies away!

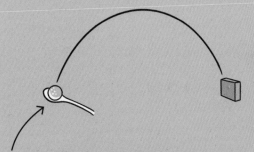

The missile will follow a curved path through air, called a trajectory. After a few tries, you can adjust how far you pull the spoon down so you hit the castle.

JUMP RAMP

Drive your toy cars off this ramp like a daredevil racer! How far can you make them fly?

For one or more people.

Ask an adult to help with cutting the box, and make sure there are no people or pets in the way when your cars are jumping.

What do you need?

- Medium-sized corrugated cardboard packing box
- Large piece of smooth, thin cardboard
- Longer corrugated cardboard packing box

- Marker pen
- Strong, sharp scissors
- Strong tape
- Toy cars

How to play

 Take the first box and carefully cut off all the flaps around the top.

 Draw a curve along one side of the box, and ask an adult to cut it out.

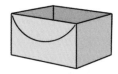

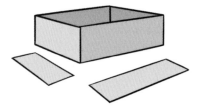

 Take the cut-out curved section and draw around it onto the other side of the box so both sides match. Then cut it out on that side too.

 Now gently curve your smooth, thin cardboard and fit it on top of the box. Trim it to fit if you need to, then tape it on to make the jump.

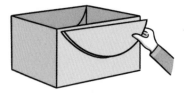

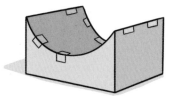

5 Lastly, you ned to add a long ramp for your cars to zoom down. Take the longer cardboard box, cut off one side, and fold up about 2.5 cm (1 in) on each side.

6 Tape one end of the ramp to the start of the jump, make the join as smooth and flat as possible, and lean the other end against a wall, table, or windowsill to make a steep slope.

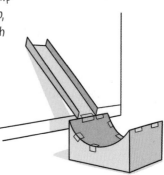

7 You're ready to roll! Hold a car near the top of the ramp, let go, and see what happens!

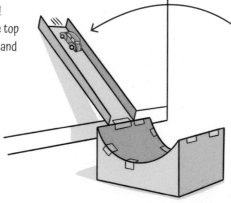

Try experimenting with starting the car at different positions on the ramp. How high does it have to be to make it jump off? Can you make it jump off, land safely, and keep going?

Wheeee!

Game science

The ramp works because of acceleration caused by gravity. When an object starts rolling or falling downhill, it moves slowly. But as it keeps falling, it keeps speeding up, or accelerating. A long ramp lets the cars pick up enough speed to fly off the jump.

MOVING MUSIC

Make an automatic music machine using a battery-powered toy train.

How to play

1 Experiment with filling jars or bottles with different amounts of water. When you hit them gently with the spoon, they will make different notes depending on how full they are.

Fun on your own or working as a team.

DING! **Ding!** **Ding!**

What do you need?

- A battery-powered toy train and train track (a larger, heavier train will work better than a tiny one)
- About ten clean glass jars or bottles (or more if you like)
- Rubber band or strong tape
- A long spoon
- Water
- Clear, empty floor space

2 Arrange a row of bottles or jars with different amounts of water in them, so they play a tune when you hit them in order. You can try to copy a tune you know, or make up your own.

3 To make your train play the bottles, you need to attach a spoon to it. If there's a clear space between the wheels, you could do this by wrapping a rubber band around the middle of the train. Fit the spoon into the rubber band so that it points backward slightly and sticks out on both sides (or use tape to hold it on).

4 Set up the train track in a straight line or circle, or any shape you like. Test your train to make sure it can run along the track without falling over. If not, adjust the spoon or try to find a lighter one.

5 Once you've got it working, line the bottles up close to the train track. Start your train so the spoon taps each bottle as it goes past, and it will play your tune!

Game science

Why does adding water to a bottle or jar make a lower note? It's because the note is made by the glass vibrating. When there's mostly air around the glass, it vibrates quickly, making a higher note. When you add more water, it can't vibrate as fast and makes a lower note.

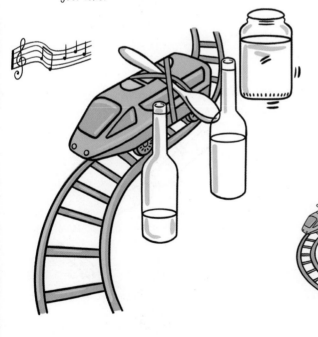

MARBLE RUN

Make your own recycled marble run from cardboard tubes.

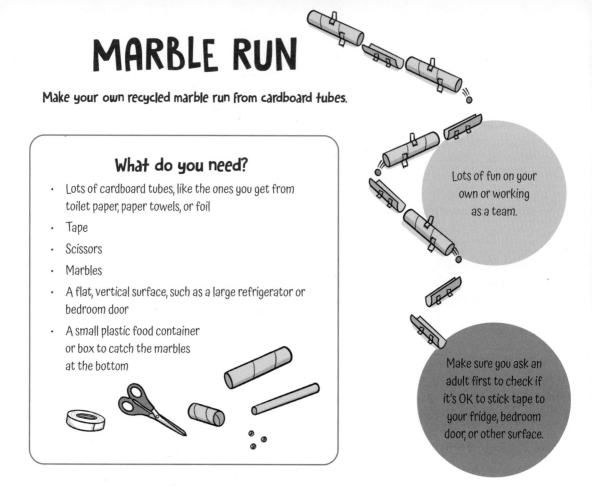

What do you need?

- Lots of cardboard tubes, like the ones you get from toilet paper, paper towels, or foil
- Tape
- Scissors
- Marbles
- A flat, vertical surface, such as a large refrigerator or bedroom door
- A small plastic food container or box to catch the marbles at the bottom

Lots of fun on your own or working as a team.

Make sure you ask an adult first to check if it's OK to stick tape to your fridge, bedroom door, or other surface.

How to play

1 The aim is to attach cardboard tubes to the surface so that when you start a marble rolling at the top, it will pass from one tube to the next, all the way to the bottom.

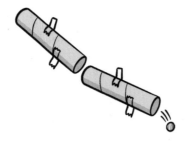

2 You can keep the tubes whole, or cut them in half to make channels.

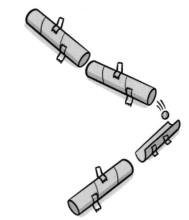

3 Leave gaps, like this ...

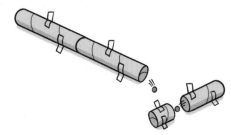

... and the fast-moving marble will jump across!

4 You can cut them to any length you like, or join two tubes together to make a longer piece.

5 Tape each piece to the surface in a sloping position, so the marble will run down it and drop into the next one.

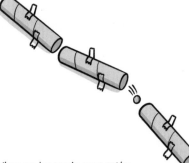

6 When you've made your entire marble run, start a marble at the top and watch it make its way down!

Game science

As you build your marble run, you'll be experimenting with gravity and how it pulls objects downhill. If you make a tube slope very gently, the marble will start rolling slower. If you use a steep slope, it will soon pick up more speed. But take care—if it's going too fast, it might jump right out! Test and adjust your design as you go.

Top tip!
Some people find it's easier to start at the bottom and work upward.

Try this too!

Can you make a marble jump across a gap?

Can you add parts that make sounds or spin around when the marble hits them?

Try using other parts too, like paper cups or cones, pipe cleaners, or string.

RUBE GOLDBERG MACHINE

Rube Goldberg was a cartoonist and sculptor who became famous for his crazy machines. A Rube Goldberg machine is a series of objects that are set up so when each one moves, it sets off the next.

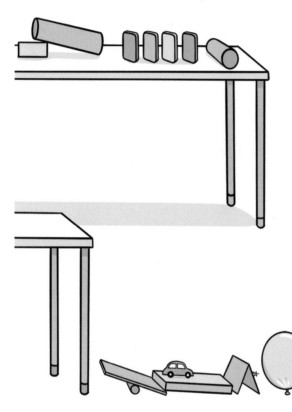

For example:

A marble rolls down a tube ...

And knocks over a domino run ...

The last domino makes a tube roll off the table ...

Landing on a seesaw, which lifts up ...

Pushing up a platform, which makes a car go down a slope ...

Which hits some cardboard with a pin on it ...

Which moves forward and pops the balloon!

What do you need?

- A clear, flat space to work in, such as an area of floor or a large tabletop
- Craft tools, such as scissors, glue, and tape
- Lots of time!

- Everyday objects and materials for making your machine parts.

  They can include:

  Paper and cardboard

  Craft sticks or popsicle sticks

  Cardboard tubes

String

Rubber bands

Paper cups

Dominoes

Toy cars

Balloons

Paper clips

Pipe cleaners

Sticky putty

Coins

Beads

Boxes and books to create different levels

Marbles

How to play

1 The great thing about Rube Goldberg machines is that what you do is up to you! Experiment with different methods and ideas for making objects move so they set off the next step in the sequence.

Ask an adult to check if it's OK to use objects and materials from around the house.

2 You can write your ideas down or sketch them on paper first, or just start building.

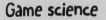

POP!

3 You may find it easier to work backward from the end of the sequence toward the beginning.

4 Keep testing your machine and tweaking the steps until it works perfectly. (It's a good idea to make a smaller machine first, with just a few steps, then move onto longer ones later.)

5 When it's ready, show it off to your friends and family. You could make a video of it too.

Game science

A Rube Goldberg machine can involve all kinds of science, including gravity, friction, acceleration, balancing, inertia, air pressure, and much more. It depends on how you build it!

Lights, camera, action!

PAPER PLANE AIR SHOW

Hold a paper plane air show and compete to make the best planes and the longest flights.

Best for up to about six players or teams.

What do you need?

- Lots of sheets of paper (re-use scrap paper if possible)
- A large indoor space
- A tape measure, pencil, and paper
- Scissors
- Tape
- Sticky tack, paper straws, or paper clips (optional)

How to play

1 First, each player or team makes their own paper planes. Allow plenty of time for trying out different designs, testing, and improving.

2 When everyone's ready, take turns flying your planes to see how far they go before hitting the floor.

Tape a paper strip to the floor for each person to stand behind when they launch a plane.

Watch where the plane lands, then measure the distance from the strip.

Game science

- Paper planes fly best if you make sure they're symmetrical (exactly the same on both sides).

- Adding a little weight to the nose of the plane (not too much!) can help it overcome air resistance and fly faster.

- Make sure there's quite a big wing area to keep the plane up.

- Try folding the back edges of the wings slightly up or down to make "ailerons". They help to control the flow of air and can affect the plane's flight.

Here are a few ideas and tips:

Type of plane

- Base your design on a classic paper dart (see page 92), a ring wing (see page 93), or a different shape, such as this bullnose plane:

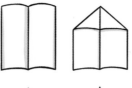

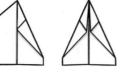

- Or create your own new shapes and designs, or mix different ideas together. For example, could you make a plane out of two ring wings, or combine a ring and a dart?

Extra materials

- If you like, use paper straws, paper clips, tape, and sticky tack too. Use them to create different designs or add weight to different areas.

Throwing style

- Don't forget to experiment with throwing methods too. If throwing hard doesn't work well, try launching your plane gently—it might go farther. You could try using the launcher on page 22, or design your own launcher.

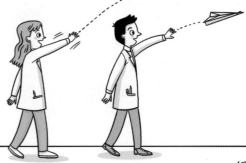

GLITTER GERMS

Germs are too small to see, which is why it's so hard to tell where they are. But what if you could see them?

Great for a large group, like a school class or a party, but you could try it at home with your family too.

Check with an adult before you do this to make sure it's okay to spread glitter around. It may be best to do this in an area that is easy to clean.

What do you need?

- Bottle of biodegradable glitter
- Handwashing sink and soap
- Unscented hand lotion
- Teaspoon

How to play

1 Choose one person to be the first to catch the germ. They should rub a drop of hand lotion on their hands, then hold out their hands while someone puts about half a teaspoon of glitter into them. Then they should rub their hands together to cover them with glitter.

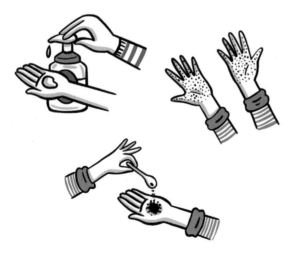

2 The glitter behaves like germs on the person's hands. When they move around, pick things up, or touch other people, they spread the germs around.

Spend 10–20 minutes doing some fun activities together. You could ...

- Play a board game.
- Build a tower of building bricks.
- Play a ball game.

3 After 10-20 minutes, check to see if you can find any of the glitter. Does anyone else have any on their hands or clothes? Can you find any on objects? Look closely, as it can be hard to spot individual glitter pieces.

4 Lastly, anyone who has glitter on their hands should try washing it off in the sink using soap and water. How long does it take to make sure every scrap of glitter is gone?

Remember to wash all over your hands, including between your fingers, your thumbs, and the backs of your hands too.

Game science

The glitter game shows you how easily germs can spread from one person to another and onto objects and surfaces where other people can pick them up. This is why it's easy to catch some types of disease germs, even if you don't go near the person who has them.

It also shows how much you have to wash your hands to really make sure all the germs are gone!

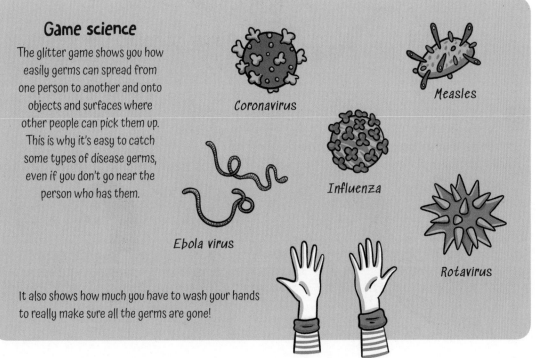

Coronavirus

Measles

Influenza

Ebola virus

Rotavirus

NEURON RACE

This game is all about the nerve cells, or neurons,
that carry signals around the brain and body.

What are neurons?

Neuron are messenger cells. When you sense things, think, make decisions,
and use your brain to control your body, signals are jumping along pathways
from one neuron to the next.

Neurons

Signals

What do you need?

- Enough space for players to stand in long rows

Best for a larger group of around 20–30 people, but you can try it with fewer.

1 Choose one person to do a test on. Explain you're going to tap them on the back, and as soon as they feel the tap, they have to clap. Stand behind them so they can't see when you're about to do it.

Tap!   Tap!

2 How fast did they do it? The time between the tap and the clap is the time it takes a signal to go from their back into their brain, for their brain to understand it, and then send signals to their hands to make them clap. To do this, signals have to pass between lots of neurons, but it happens very quickly. Try it on a few other people too.

The nervous system includes the brain and the nerves that reach all over the body, connecting your brain to all your body parts. It's made of neurons that carry signals

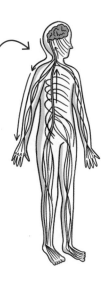

In most people, this will take much less than a second.

3 Now for the neuron race. Divide your group into two equal teams (if there's an odd number, take turns so everyone can play). Each team should stand in a row, facing forward, so each person is looking at the back of the person in front.

4 On the count of three, the person at the start of each row should tap the next person's back. As soon as they feel it, they should tap the next person's back, and so on.

Which team can pass the signal the fastest?

No cheating! Only tap when you feel a tap!

Game science

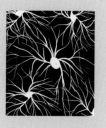

In this game, you're using the speed of your neurons to race. But the row of people also acts like a chain of neurons, with each person passing the signal on to the next.

E.S.P. TEST

E.S.P. is short for extra-sensory perception. It means things like being able to read someone's mind or knowing where something is hidden without any information or clues.

Of course, most people would say that's impossible—but some people claim they can do it. So scientists have invented tests to see if it's really true.

What do you need?

- Plain cardboard
- Scissors
- Marker pens
- Pen and paper

You need at least three people but a bigger group is better so you can do more tests.

How to play

1 Cut out 10 equal-sized pieces of cardboard, about the size of playing cards. Make two sets of five cards and decorate each set with these five different designs (on one side only).

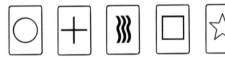

2 To play, two people face away from each other while another keeps score.

3 Give each player a set of cards. One player holds theirs in their hand face down. The other player puts their cards in front of them, face up.

4 To play, the scorekeeper says "Card 1" and writes "1" on their paper.

5 The first player chooses a card at random and looks at it. Then they have to try to "send" that picture to the other player, using their thoughts!

Here comes the message!

6 The other player has to guess which card the first player is looking at.

7 The scorekeeper writes down what the card really was, as well as the guess.

8 Then repeat this at least ten times. Each time, the first player puts back the last card, shuffles the cards, and chooses again.

Card	Guess
1. Square	Star
2. Water	Square
3. Cross	Water
4. Cross	Star
5. Circle	Circle
6. Star	Cross
7. Square	Star
8. Water	Water
9. Square	Star
10. Water	Water

Game science

If people really could read minds or send messages using their brains, you would expect to see some higher scores, like 7 out of 10. However, when scientists have done this test, they've found that the results are what you would expect by chance—suggesting that people don't really have ESP.

If someone gets a high score, it could also be because they're getting some kind of clue. For example, can they hear what the scorekeeper is writing? Make sure you check every possibility!

9 Then check the results! There's a one in five chance the guess will be right each time. So you would expect around two of the answers to be right.

To be really sure, you need to repeat the test several times and try it on different pairs of people.

PROGRAM A ROBOT

Get a friend to act as a robot and write a program to make them do a task.

Your wish is my command!

For any size group. Work together to do the programming, and take turns being the robot.

What do you need?

- Empty floor space
- Table
- Small object, such as a coin
- A few unbreakable objects to use as obstacles, such as stools or large cardboard boxes
- Pen and paper
- Scarf or bandanna to use as a blindfold

How to play

1. Ask the robot to leave the room so they don't see the task.

2. At one end of the space, put the coin or other small object on the table. Set up a simple obstacle course in the room so the robot will have to walk around obstacles to reach the coin.

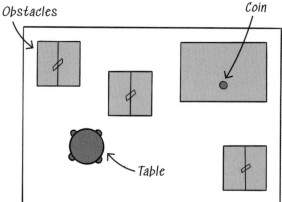

Obstacles

Coin

Table

3 Set a starting position, such as a mark on the floor.

 4 Then figure out all the instructions a robot would need to start at the starting point, avoid the obstacles, reach the table, and pick up the coin. Write them down in a list, like lines of computer code.

Go forward 3 steps

Turn to the right

Go forward 2 steps

Turn to the left

Go forward 2 steps

Turn to the left

Go forward 3 steps

Game science

When we program computers and robots, we have to give them complete, clear instructions. Without these, they can't do anything. If the code has a problem, or a bug, the computer or robot won't work. So programmers have to make sure they think of everything and make the instructions work in the right order. You might need more instructions than you think!

5 When you're happy with your program, blindfold the robot, stand them at the starting point, and read out the code line by line for them to follow.

 6 If the robot hits an obstacle or fails to get the coin, the code has a bug!

7 Keep changing and testing the code until it works.

DANCE CODING

Be a computer choreographer! Create a simple coding language for dance moves, then test it out.

For any size group.

What do you need?

- A space you can dance in
- Music and something to play it on
- Pen and paper

How to play

1 Think of three or four simple dance moves and give each move a number, such as:

1. Jump   2. Nod   3. Wave   4. Clap

2 Listen to the music you want to dance to, and create a pattern of different moves to make a dance. Write the pattern down on paper, with each move going with one beat of the music.

3 To do a move more than once, use a multiplication sign.

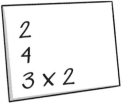

2
4
3 × 2

4 To repeat a section, add an arrow with a multiplication sign and the number of repetitions.

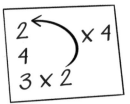

2
4   × 4
3 × 2

5 Keep going until you have a whole dance routine.

6 Then see if everyone in the group can follow the code to do the dance to the music together.

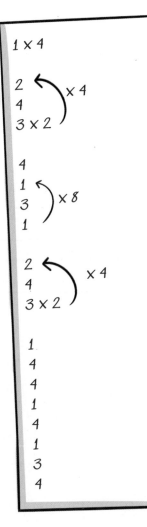

```
1 × 4

2
4   × 4
3 × 2

4
1
3   × 8
1

2
4   × 4
3 × 2

1
4
4
1
4
1
3
4
```

Try this too!

If you like doing this, you could try a more complicated version where different people or groups of people have different instructions to follow.

Game science

Real computer programs use lists of instructions like this, with loops to repeat sections of code, saving space and time. Can you work out ways to code more complicated things too? What if you wanted to do two dance moves at the same time, for example? See if you can invent new symbols or instructions for doing useful things.

ELEMENT BINGO

Elements are the pure, basic materials that everything is made from, such as hydrogen, oxygen, carbon, or silver. This bingo game helps you remember their names and symbols.

For groups of 5–10 people, plus a bingo caller. You will need a bingo card for each player.

What do you need?

- Cardboard
- Scissors
- Ruler
- Cup
- Pen and paper
- A pencil for each player
- The list of elements below

THE FIRST 20 ELEMENTS

- H—Hydrogen
- He—Helium
- Li—Lithium
- Be—Beryllium
- B—Boron
- C—Carbon
- N—Nitrogen
- O—Oxygen
- F—Fluorine
- Ne—Neon
- Na—Sodium
- Mg—Magnesium
- Al—Aluminum (or aluminium)
- Si—Silicon
- P—Phosphorus
- S—Sulfur
- Cl—Chlorine
- Ar—Argon
- K—Potassium
- Ca—Calcium

 First, make your bingo cards. Draw and cut out a piece of cardboard for each player, about 12 cm (5 in) long and 7 cm (3 in) wide. Draw a grid of nine rectangles on each card.

 Now you need a list of 20 elements. You can use our list of the first 20 elements, or look up other elements and make your own list.

Use a black pen to fill in each card with a different selection of elements. Try to make sure no two cards have the exact same elements on them.

O–Oxygen	B–Boron	Ar–Argon
S–Sulphur	Ne–Neon	He–Helium
Na–Sodium	Si–Silicon	C–Carbon

L–Lithium	Ne–Neon	Be–Beryllium
Na–Sodium	F–Fluorine	O–Oxygen
H–Hydrogen	C–Carbon	Cl–Chlorine

 Now write down each element in your list on paper, cut them up into separate elements, and put them in the cup.

Each element has its own symbol.

5. To play the game, give each person a bingo card and a pencil.

6. The caller picks an element out of the cup and reads it out loud. If a player has that element on their card, they cross it off.

L - Lithium	Ne - Neon	Be - Beryllium
Na - Sodium	F - Fluorine	O - Oxygen
H - Hydrogen	C - Carbon	Cl - Chlorine

It's elemental!

7. The caller keeps doing this, taking the elements out of the cup one by one.

BINGOOOOOOO!

8. Eventually, one person will have crossed off all the elements on their card. They shout BINGO! and win the game!

Game science

Elements can exist on their own, like the gold in a gold ring. Or they can combine to make other substances—for example, water is made of oxygen and hydrogen. Understanding elements is central to the science of chemistry, which explores what materials are made of and how they behave.

SPACE BINGO

For a space bingo game, follow the instructions for element bingo, but with the names of planets, moons, and stars instead. Here's a list of 20 you could use:

SPACE BINGO LIST

· Sun	· Mars	· Pluto	· Callisto
· Moon	· Jupiter	· Sedna	· Europa
· Earth	· Saturn	· Titan	· Enceladus
· Mercury	· Uranus	· Io	· Triton
· Venus	· Neptune	· Ganymede	· Charon

POLLEN RACE

If you have hayfever, you'll know that pollen blows around in the wind.
It's trying to make its way from one flower to another, to make seeds grow.

How to play

1 Draw a large flower, about 30 cm (12 in) across, on the newspaper or wrapping paper and cut it out. Draw around this flower onto more paper to make more flowers all the same shape and size, one for each team or player.

For up to four players or small teams of two or three people.

What do you need?

- Tissue paper
- Thin books or pieces of thick cardboard (one each)
- Old newspaper or wrapping paper
- Pen
- Large coin
- Scissors
- Removable tape
- A large, clear floor area

2 Put the flowers in a row at one end of your floor area, space them evenly apart, and use a bit of tape to attach them to the floor. Mark each flower with a number.

3 Make lots of small paper circles by drawing around the coin onto the tissue paper and cutting the circles out. This is your pollen! Make four circles for each player or team.

4 To race, line up each team or player at the other end of the space, opposite a flower. Each team should put their pollen circles on the floor in front of them, and each person should have a book or piece of card.

5 On the count of three, each player or team has to blow all their pollen circles onto their flower by flapping their book or cardboard. The winner is the one who gets all their pollen pieces on their flower first. (Or if some pollen gets lost, the team with the most!)

Take care! If you flap too hard your pollen won't go the right way.

Game science

Many plants rely on the wind to spread their pollen—but the wind often doesn't carry it to the right place. Because of this, plants release a lot of pollen so there's a good chance some of it will reach the target.

That's why the air is full of pollen in summer, making people sneeze!

CAMOUFLAGE GAME

Create perfectly camouflaged animals and challenge your friends or family to find them.

What do you need?

- An internet-linked computer and printer. If you don't have a computer, you could find the pictures you need in an old travel or wildlife magazine. Ask first if it's OK to cut it up!
  - Pencil
  - Scissors
  - Glue

Ask an adult if you can use the computer and printer, and ask them for help finding good photos.

For up to about ten people.

How to play

1. Use the internet to find several clear, detailed, close-up pictures of different wild places, such as:

A thick jungle

A sandy desert

A savanna with long grass

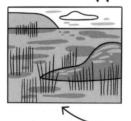

A leafy forest floor

Look for pictures with lots of detail and texture.

2. Choose a picture and print four copies of it.

3 Divide your group into two teams, and give each team two copies. Working separately, so they can't see each other, each team has to use one of their pictures to make some small animal shapes, like these. Draw them on the picture first, then carefully cut them out carefully.

4 Then each team should hide their animals on the other printout, trying to make them as invisible as possible. Use a dot of glue to hold them in place, so they don't move around. Smooth down the cut edges and position them in the area you cut them from for the best results!

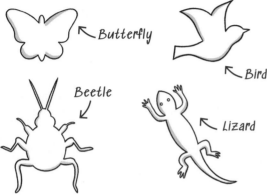

← Butterfly

← Bird

Beetle

← Lizard

What are you looking at?

5 Now each team has to spot the other team's camouflaged animals. Who can get them all first?

Game science

Many animals have brilliant camouflage. They match their surroundings to make it hard for hunters to spot them. We often can't see them either, even in closeup photos!

EARTH AND THE MOON

How far away is the Moon from the Earth? See how close your guess is.

For up to about
30 players

What do you need?

- White paper or card
- Marker pens
- Compass
- Scissors
- Removable tape
- Large room
- Tape measure
- Calculator

How to play

1 First, make your Earth. Draw a circle on your paper or cardboard that's exactly 20 cm (8 in) in diameter and cut it out. You can decorate it to look like the Earth, or just write "Earth" on it.

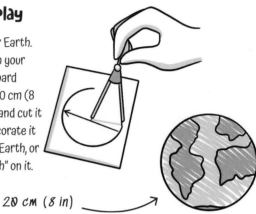

20 cm (8 in)

2 Next, make lots of Moons, one for each player. Draw a circle exactly 5.5 cm (2.2 in) across, cut it out, then draw around it to make more Moons.

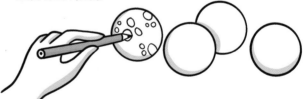

3 These Earth and Moon models are to scale, meaning they are the right sizes compared to each other. In real life, they are this big:

Earth diameter:
12,742 km
(7,918 mi)

Moon diameter:
3,475 km (2,159 mi) — or just over $\frac{1}{4}$ of the width of the Earth

But how far are apart are they?

 4 Put the Earth on the floor at one end of the room, and hold it still with a bit of tape.

 5 Get everyone to write their name or initials on their Moon, then put them the distance from the Earth they think it would be if the Earth and the Moon were these sizes.

6 When everyone has put their Moon in place, figure out the answer!

20 × 30.2

7 The distance to the Moon varies slightly as it moves around, but on average it's about 384,400 km (238,855 mi). This distance is about 30.2 times the Earth's diameter.

Your Earth is 20 cm (8 in) wide. Multiply this by 30.2 to give you the distance away your model Moon should be, and use the tape measure to measure it out on the ground.

Game science

Were you surprised? Your answer should be a distance of about 6 m (20 ft). Most people guess the Moon is much closer than this. That's probably because diagrams often make it look closer, and it also looks quite close when we see it in the sky.

In reality, the Moon and the Earth look like this in space:

Earth   Moon

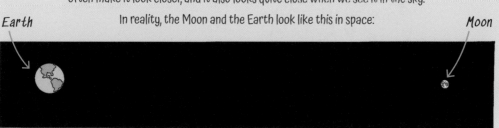

GLOSSARY

Acceleration Speeding up, or getting faster.

Acid A substance with a pH of less than 7. The opposite of alkaline.

Adenine One of the four strands in DNA.

Aileron A raised hinge on a wing, used to control how the aircraft flies.

Air pressure How much weight air has.

Air resistance A force that happens when an object moves through the air. The air pulls against the object.

Alkaline A substance with a pH of more than 7. The opposite of acid.

Aristotle An ancient Greek philosopher and scientist, who examined how the world worked.

Artificial Human-made, not natural.

Atom The smallest chemical building blocks.

Balance When an object's weight is evenly spread, allowing it to stay upright and steady.

Camouflage Shades and textures that allow an object or animal to blend into its surroundings.

Catamaran A type of boat.

Cell The smallest building blocks of all living things.

Code (computer) A series of instructions used to tell a computer or robot what to do.

Coding language A special language spoken by computers and robots, which programmers use to tell the computer what to do.

Constellation A collection of stars in the night sky that appear to make a pattern or shape.

Coronavirus A type of virus that can make you unwell.

Cytosine One of the four strands in DNA.

Density How close together the molecules in an object are.

DNA Deoxyribonucleic acid. Chains of cells which carry instructions for a living thing.

Ebola virus A type of virus that can make you unwell.

Element A substance that is made up of one type of atom.

ESP Extrasensory perception. The idea that a person can predict what is going to happen using a "sixth sense."

Forces Rules that can change how an object moves.

Friction The resistance when one object rubs against another.

Germ A tiny living thing that can live inside another living thing.

Gravity The force that makes objects fall toward the Earth.

Guanine One of the four strands in DNA.

Horizontal Parallel to the ground.

Inertia When an object isn't moving.

Influenza A type of virus that can make you unwell.

Isaac Newton A scientist who discovered the force of gravity.

John Ridley Stroop A scientist who discovered the Stroop Effect.

Kinetic energy Movement energy.

Lever A long, solid object that moves around a set point, called a pivot.

Long-term memory Remembering things from a long time ago.

Magnet A material that attracts other materials toward it.

Measles A type of virus that can make you unwell.

Molecule A group of atoms bonded together.

Nerve A group of long, threadlike structures that carry messages to and from your brain.

Neuron Cells which send messages from the senses to the brain.

Newton's cradle A toy which shows how kinetic energy moves between objects.

Pendulum A weight hung from a fixed point that swings from side to side.

pH A measurement of how acid or alkaline something is.

Positive reinforcement A way of training a person or animal to do something, using praise.

Program (computer) A series of instructions that tell a computer what to do.

Rotavirus A type of virus that can make you unwell.

Rube Goldberg An artist who invented the Rube Goldberg machine.

Rube Goldberg machine A complicated contraption that involves a chain reaction of different actions.

Short-term memory Remembering something that has happened recently.

Spacewalk When an astronaut goes outside a spacecraft, wearing a space suit.

Stroop Effect When your brain is presented with different information, leading to a delay in processing the information. For example, if you see the word "blue" written in green, it will take your brain longer to read the word than if the word had been written in blue.

Surface area The area of the outside part of something.

Surface tension When all the particles on the outside layer of something stick together

Symmetry When both sides of something are mirror images of one another.

Thymine One of the four strands in DNA.

Trajectory The path followed by a moving object.

Wavelength How close together or far apart a light wave is.

Vertical Running from top to bottom.

Vibration When the particles of an object move very quickly.

Viscosity How thick a liquid is.

Vortex When liquid or air whirls together around a mid-point.